3.9 Media and general public 89
3.10 Stakeholders 92
3.11 Corporate culture 96
3.12 Resource constrains 99
3.13 Market analysis 102
3.14 Swot analysis 105

Chapter 4: Evaluate what is critical 112
4.1 Target market selection 114
4.2 Market strategies, building a competitive advantage 117
4.3 Product strategies – review product and company life cycle status 120
4.4 Relationship strategies – consider building relationship maps 124
4.5 Competitive strategies 128
4.6 Brand strategies – building value 131
4.7 Positioning strategies – company, brand, products and services 134

Chapter 5: Construct and Implement the strategic plan 140
5.1 Elements of a strategic plan 140
5.2 Implementation 143
    5.2.1 Barriers to effective implementation 144
    5.2.2 Successful plan implementation 147
    5.2.3 Methods to improve strategy implementation 150
5.3 Control 153

Chapter 6: Review, manage successes and take corrective action   159
6.1 Review for results   159
6.2 Manage for success   160
6.3 Celebrate your successes   161
6.4 Taking corrective action   162

Recommended Reading and Viewing – QR Codes   165

"So What's your Plan?"

"Vision without action is a daydream. Action without vision is a nightmare"
Japanese proverb

Having a plan allows you the opportunity to influence the future. If you do not have a plan or would like to improve on your current plan, then use this practical workbook to formulate a business plan for your future

First published in 2017 by - 4Vision4Growth
Johannesburg

Practical and Informative Workbooks, enables readers to complete tasks or worksheets or discussions in a short space of time yet derive maximum practical and intellectual value.

Copyright © Gerhard van Wyk 2017

The right of Gerhard van Wyk to be identified as the Author of this Work has been asserted by him in accordance with the Copyright Act No.98 of 1978 as amended up to Copyright Amendment Act 2002.
This book is sold subject to the condition that it shall not, by way of trade or otherwise, be lent, resold, hired out, or otherwise circulated without the publisher's prior written consent in any form of binding or cover other than that in which it is published and without a similar condition, including this condition being imposed on the subsequent purchaser.

Cover and text illustrations by 4Vision4Growth Creations

Printed and bound by CreateSpace
ISBN – 9781792907234

Available from Amazon.com, CreateSpace.com, on Kindle and other devices including selected retail outlets

CONTENT

About the Author	5
Preface	6
Acknowledgements	7

Chapter 1: What's in a plan? 10

Chapter 2: Vision, Mission and Objectives 19
2.1 Vision 19
2.2 Mission 22
2.3 Clarify objectives 26
    2.3.1 Barriers to achieving business plan objectives 31

Chapter 3: Understand the current position 37
3.1 Macro environmental analysis (external) 40
    3.1.1 Economy 43
    3.1.2 Government (Policy's) 46
    3.1.3 Technology 50
    3.1.4 Legal 53
    3.1.5 Social and Cultural conditions 56
    3.1.6 Nature (Environmental) 60
3.2 Micro environmental analysis (internal analysis) 64
3.3 Industry 67
3.4 Customers 70
3.5 Suppliers 74
3.6 Competitors 78
3.7 Distribution channels 83
3.8 Employees 86

About the Author

Dr Gerhard van Wyk's area of expertise relates to Marketing and Sales Management with specific focus on Business to Business Marketing, Sales and Franchising. Gerhard's working experience exceeds twenty-five years in the petrochemical and chemical sectors. He is involved in the identification of growth opportunities and the development of marketing and sales strategies to unlock sustainable wealth. Being a part time academic Gerhard lectures Marketing and Sales Management and supervise the creation and completion of dissertations for MBA students. Gerhard is also an accomplished author of several academic and other articles on Marketing, Sales, B2B and Franchising.

His publications appear regularly in local newspapers, magazines and on social media platforms. He has featured on radio and television programmes discussing marketing, sales, advertising, personal goal setting and the value of having a business plan.

The Big Small Business Show - Expert Interview with Dr Gerhard van Wyk on Marketing and Strategy - **So What`s your Plan?** - 2017
https://www.youtube.com/watch?v=xPr__bmjiuI

The Big Small Business Show - Expert Interview with Dr Gerhard van Wyk on the importance of doing a Situation Analysis
https://www.youtube.com/watch?v=JGLHhiivw-8

The Big Small Business Show - Expert Interview with Dr Gerhard van Wyk on Differentiation and its importance
https://www.youtube.com/watch?v=eAZ6C1eCTdI

The Big Small Business Show- Expert Interview with Dr Gerhard van Wyk on Differentiating your business from others
https://www.youtube.com/watch?v=lGeiPWnO1Yk

Author's favourite quote: "You might not be able to change your circumstances but you can always change your attitude" Follow us on **Twitter**: @4Vision4Growth or
Youtube: https://t.co/R5LJAd5nKx

Preface

In my discussion with many business owners and entrepreneurs over the years, I have often asked the question - how did you start the business or how were you able to identify the opportunities and capitalise on them? Some share stories of luck being at the right place at the right time and other share some amazing insights of dedication and hard work. However, after further analyses it became clear that these individuals as existing or aspiring entrepreneurs had one thing in common – **They had a Plan!**

Granted not all plans were formal or even sophisticated (not that having a formal or sophisticated plan is a guarantee for success) but they had a workable plan that identified opportunities and drove activities. Whether you are an existing or aspirational entrepreneur, making use of this workbook will guide and assist you in formulating your thoughts and actions in order to identify opportunities and to grow your business. I am excited that you have decided to read this book. **So What's your Plan?** Can change your live for the better and you in turn can change the lives of others, one plan at a time.

Acknowledgements

I would like to acknowledge my wife Dunè and children, Dominik and Ludwik for their continued support and encouragement in everything I do. To those who have allowed me to be part of their dreams of starting a new business, growing existing businesses, identifying opportunities and formulating strategies to capitalise on, identified opportunities over the years, thank you. Not only have I been able to work with some of the best marketing and sales people in the industry but I have also been fortunate to consolidate the practical and theoretical aspects of business through real projects and applications. To the collective who have mentored and gone ahead of me - I have taken your inputs and knowledge in formulation with my own understandings and experience and are hoping to share these insights with all potential and current entrepreneurs that have a **Vision for Growth**. Simply follow the *SWYP-methodology* to create massively successful strategic plans for your business and your life !

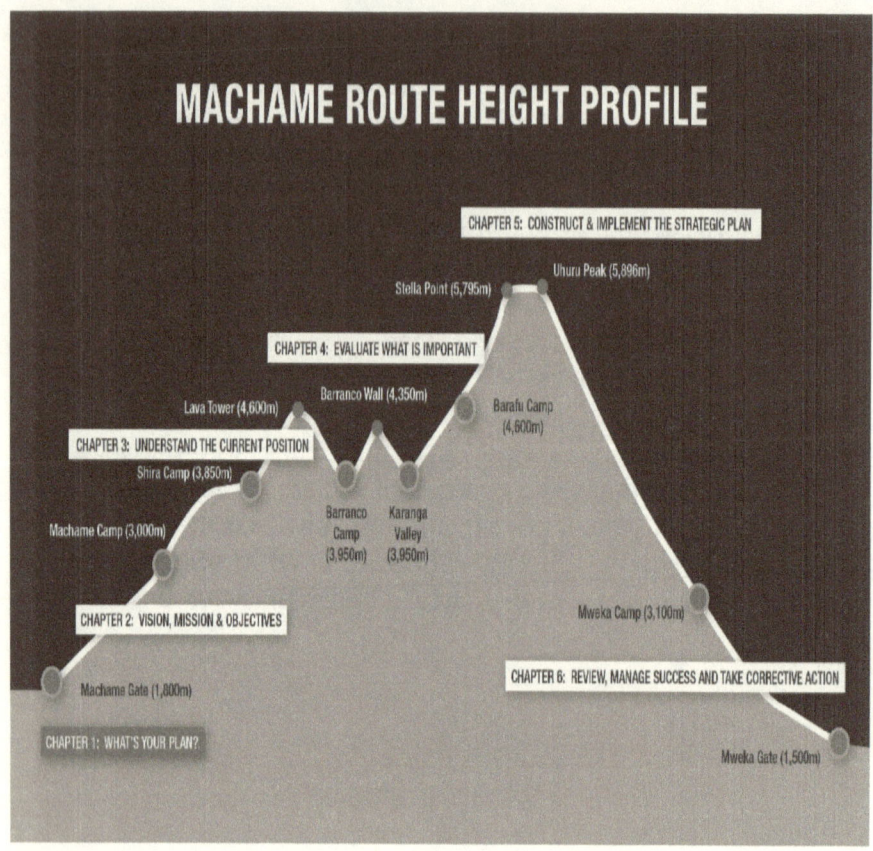

Personal Journey: Machame Route

*When I decided to climb Kilimanjaro I was confronted with many plans and potential routes already attempted by others to reach the highest point in Africa: **5,895** meters above sea level. My selection of the route was mostly influenced by the detail of the plan and route presented as a measure of the difficulty of the route and in my mind my potential to reach the top. Please follow my personal day-to-day journey of reaching the top and returning safely to a place of comfort at the foot of the mountain by following a well-formulated and structured plan. The Machame route is a wilderness route, which combines spectacular views and scenery and good acclimatisation.*

With a gradual ascend through the forest you emerge to see wide views of the moorland on Shira plateau, rocky trails and scree with stunning scenery and beautiful ice formations along the way. The different kinds of vegetation found along the route makes it the most scenic route. For all these reasons, it is perhaps the best of the standard routes on the mountain. Overnight are spent camping in tents.

Day 1 on mountain
Machame Gate – Machame Camp 1,828m (5,997ft) – 3,032m (9,948ft)
Average hiking time: 7 hours
Before embarking on the hike a compulsory park register must be signed by each climber. The path follows a ridge through dense mountain forest. This is the most richly forested area on the mountain, and the zone from where 96 % of the water on Kilimanjaro originates. This area is very lush and beautiful on sunny days and especially during the dry season. It can also be a very muddy experience, particularly after recent rains! We had lunch at 'Halfway Clearing', a small opening in the trees, and continued climbing steadily. The gradient becomes gentler as the forest slowly merges into a giant heather close to the Machame Camp. We may get our first closer look at the glacial dome of Kibo if the evening clouds permit. **Overnight at Machame Camp**

Chapter 1: What's in a plan?

"By failing to prepare, you are preparing to fail"
Benjamin Franklin (1706-1790) American statesman, scientist and philosopher.

With or without a plan of action, people all over the world achieve great things and move from strength to strength; however, on average having a plan and implementing it improves the success rate dramatically of moving from a current state to a desired state. In the absence of planning, most activities on a personal or business level become meaningless. Planning gives focus, direction and assist with the clarification of where we are now (how did we get here), what to do (where are we heading), how to do it, when to do it, who needs to do it and why it needs to be done. It is just logic to have a plan. A plan starts at a point and has some iteration in between the start and the end, but normally ends at a selected or desired destination. Below is one such suggested plan to reach the highest point in Africa, the summit of Mount Kilimanjaro.

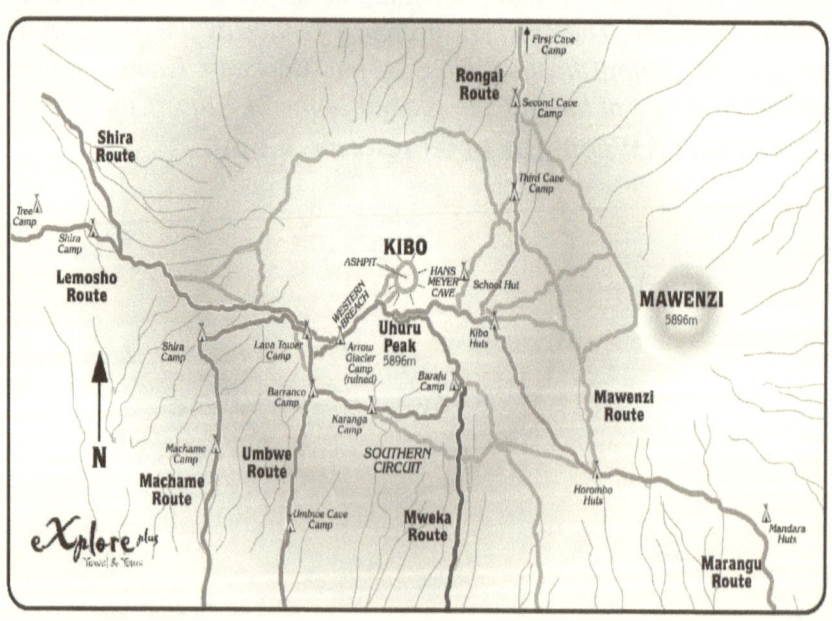

The Machame six-day route is one suggested route to travel but many others will also lead you to the top, however as a novice mountain climber I am sure you will agree having a map or plan with some information is better than hoping to summit with no plan or insight to the task at hand? Most people dream of achieving great things in live, we all have our personal objectives and some might even have business objectives. It is safe to assume that most people could also share stories of missed objectives, dreams or aspirations. This is normal and happens to all of us. In order to increase our success, rate we need to understand a few things that could assist us on this journey to improve our chances.

Do

Starting a planning process will be supported by first defining your personal and business goals. Writing down and understanding your goals will guide you on what it will take to achieve these goals and over which period? It is best to divide your goals into short-term (12 months), medium-term (2-3 years) and long-term goals (4-5years).

	Goals	**Short term**	**Medium term**	**Long term**
1				
2				
3				
4				
5				

Hold onto your objectives as set out above, as we develop a more comprehensive understanding of planning and implementation in later chapters you will be able to reflect on your original goals and see if they meet the criteria for smart objectives. Having a plan or a thought process of moving from one place or position to another is not something new, even in ancient times many Kings, leaders and laymen followed a plan of action.

So What's your Plan?

Think of the early explorers, they had maps of routes travelled or lands explored by others and had some plan of how to execute activities on their journey. Things such as which ship will they use, who will be the crew, what skills must they have, do they have money for the exploration if not who will fund them, will they need arms to protect themselves, what about food and clean drinking water. Those early explorers were brave and well-travelled men with a high degree of knowledge about risk due to many uncertain factors. Risk is a completely different energy that often assists with the execution of a plan and we will talk about the importance of managing and mitigating risk later. For the purpose of improving our likelihood of successfully moving from point A to B we need a plan. If we have direction, clarity of purpose and a better understanding of the journey with regards to risk we could influence others to join us and assist in reaching our dreams.

Watch: Is a Business Plan Any Use? – YouTube
If you had any doubts regarding the value of having a plan watch this 6-minute video from Cranfield University's School of Management, **Is a Business Plan Any Use?**
https://www.youtube.com/watch?v=3jK25e8cJA4

(1)

Would you build a house without a plan?

Most people won't and I would advise you to make sure you have a plan before you start! Why? I believe you would have too many variables not accounted for and most importantly, you might find it difficult to convince the bank to loan you the money to build your dream house without a plan to demonstrate your end result.

Having to take others along on the journey, specifically those who you need to invest in your dream will take some convincing and explanation. One of the ways to do this is to have a plan and share it with your stakeholders. This will clearly explain what geographical area you plan to build your house in, what is the cost of the land, what is the size of the house, how many rooms, bathrooms, garages and who will build the house etcetera.

When do you plan to start the project and when do you plan to move in? What kind of finishes will be used, who will be the owner, and does the building plan comply with all the building standards and bylaws? What is the value of other properties in the area? Do you know how to obtain a building loan from the bank, how can you draw against the loan and what are the securities you need to provide? Who is the architect and what are the fees associated with the project? Who will manage the project? Have you budgeted for a project manager or will you be running the project? In short, before achieving your objective of building a house you need to do some homework in understanding a few important things that will assist in the execution of your dreams. All plans start with a dream and all dreams start with a plan! For the less complicated things in live perhaps neither are needed, you decide.

Below are a few examples of house plans – it is clear that it's complicated and helps to take care of most of the variables to give direction and manage the risk during the execution phase of the project. It also assists with the costing of the project.

Basic House Plan

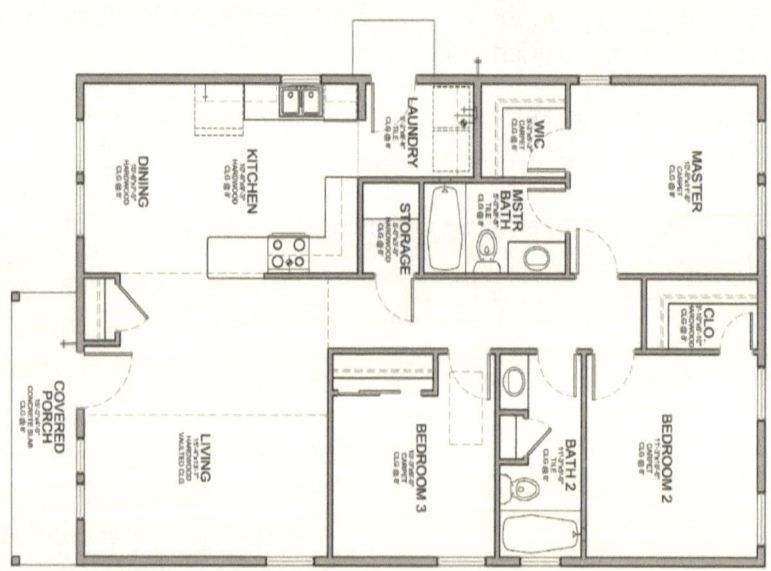

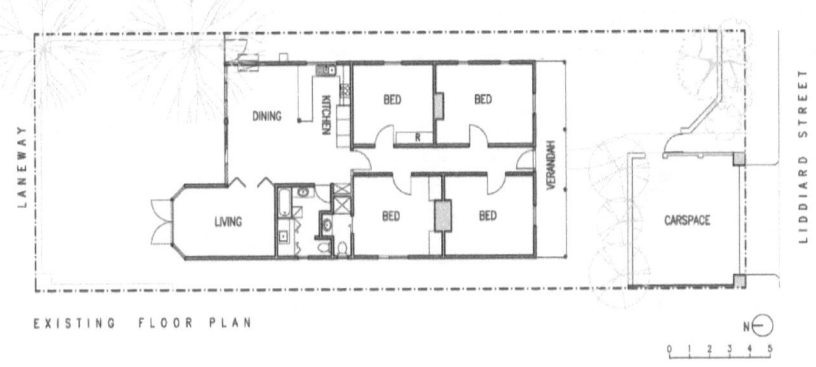

Looking at the basic house plan as illustrated, it displays a level of complexity but also assists in creating direction with some mental picture of what the end-result might look like.

Read

Read and enjoy an article written by Mark Henricks "Do You Really Need a Business Plan?"
https://www.entrepreneur.com/article/198618

(2)

Also read: Start a Business in 7 Days – James Caan. In this book James explain the importance of having a plan but that a plan without action is not a plan at all.

Going forward we will focus on the process of developing and implementing a strategic plan applicable to a business environment. This would be useful for entrepreneurs, franchisors, franchisees, small and medium enterprises, marketing and sales people and all others interested parties in moving from a current state to a desired state.

Debate

Review your current position and understand if you are content with it to remain as it is. Otherwise, does your organisation have a desire to move from the current position to an alternative position? If yes, do you know what that position is and what moving to the desired position will mean for yourself, your business and potentially your shareholders and employees? Do you have a plan for getting from where you are to the desired destination? If yes, what is the condition of the plan, when last was it updated, is it still relevant? If you do not have a plan, who is responsible for the plan and by when is it needed. What sort of a plan is needed, short-term, medium-term or a long-term plan?

5 - Point plan

Potential points to consider before constructing a plan:
- Where are we as a business? Always have an understanding of your current position relative to the industry you operate in, what your revenue will be, the product ranges you will stock etcetera.
- How did we get here? Always have a good understanding on how you got to your current position, what were the main drivers and or contributors.
- Where do we want to go? Always have a clear understanding of where you would like to be – the desired position.
- What do we have to do to get to the desired position? Always have a clear and realistic understanding of what it will take to get to the desired position, for example; infrastructure, people, training or capital.

- Do we have the strategic leadership to get to the desired position? Leaders hoping to effect change needs to lead from the front, be strategic and create an environment for teams to be creative.

"It is not the strongest of the species that survive, not the most intelligent, but the one most responsive to change"
Charles Darwin

So What's your Plan?

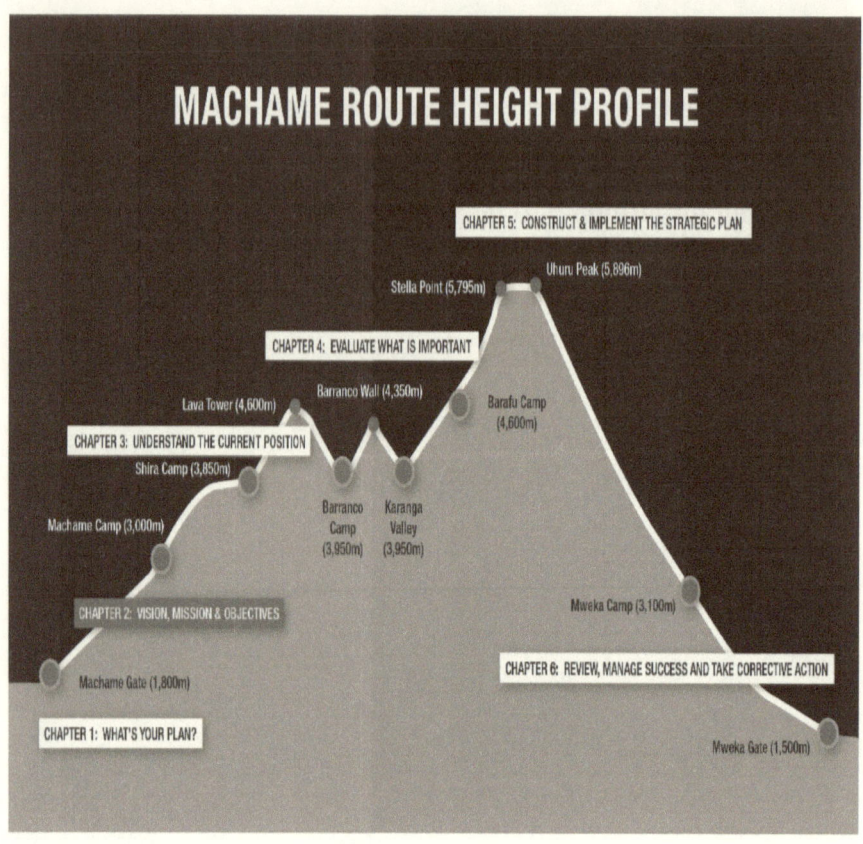

Personal Journey: Machame Camp – Shira Camp
Day 2 on mountain
Machame Camp – Shira camp 3,032m (9,948ft) – 3,847m (12,621ft)

Average hiking time: 5 hours

A shorter day that starts with a steep climb to reach a small semi-circular cliff known as Picnic Rock. There are excellent views of Kibo and the jagged rim of Shira Plateau from here, and it is a good resting point too! The trail continues less steeply to reach the Shira Plateau. We camp at Shira Camp, which has some of the most stunning views of Kilimanjaro.

Here we are close to the huge volcanic cone of Kibo and the spectacular rock formations of Shira Plateau with an unforgettable view of Mount Meru floating on the clouds. **Overnight at Shira Camp**

Chapter 2: Vision, Mission and Objectives

"Leadership is working with goals and vision; management is working with objectives"

Russel Honore

Before starting any business or exploring the opportunity to formulate a business or marketing plan, take time and read the vision and mission statements of others in the same industry. Entrepreneurs starting out are often so eager to start that they do not make time to begin at the beginning. Unfortunately, if you do not have clarity of your business vision and mission statements, do you realistically expect others to support and follow your dreams? Taking time to clarify business vision and mission statements will save time in the end and assist with the clarification of activities.

2.1 Vision

Do not underestimate the power of a vision? McDonald's founder, Ray Kroc, pictured his empire long before it existed, and he saw how to get there. He invented the company motto – 'Quality, service, cleanliness and value' – and kept repeating it to employees for the rest of his life.
Kenneth Labich

Why do you need a vision and what is the value of a vision to others? Many people fail to see the value of a vision statement, however in short if you are unable to visualise your aspirations and dreams how do you expect others to support you in achieving them? In business stakeholders, entrepreneurs and team members continuously look for guidance and direction, a dream to believe in. This directs activities and ensures everyone has the same dreams and aspirations. Entrepreneurs are good examples of people with vision. They tend to see and experience potential opportunities long before others, but sometimes have difficulty in getting others to support their efforts.

Debate

Review your current vision and determine if it is still relevant and applicable to your business activities. If you do not have a vision, spend some time with your team members and stakeholders to formulate a vision for yourself and your organisation. Once done debate and share it with others in your industry and of course with your customers.

During the refining process, you will temper the vision statement to be reflective of your aspirations. Print it in bold and communicate it to all interested parties – make sure everyone understands your vision and that all activities are aligned to support the vision. This will also be the starting point for the formulation of your strategic plan.

It is important to clarify the purpose of the strategic plan by formulating a vision statement. What is your personal and business vision? You should be able to contextualise this in a few words. A vision statement adds the 'why' and 'how' to a company's mission statement. As a company grows, its objectives and goals may change. Therefore, vision statements should be reviewed and adjusted as needed to reflect the changing business culture as goals are met. Examples of some corporate vision statements:

Mazda- Vision: To create new value, excite and delight our customers through the best automotive products and services.

Pfizer – Vision: We will become the world's most valued company to patients, customers, colleagues, investors, business partners, and the communities where we work and live.

Robert Bosch Corporation – Vision: Invented for Life. Enhance the quality of life with solutions that are both innovative and beneficial.

Wal-Mart - Vision: Saving people money to help them live better was the goal that Sam Walton envisioned when he opened the doors to the first Walmart more than 40 years ago. Today, this mission is more important than ever to our customers and members around the world.

Watch:  **How to Write a Great Business Vision Statement - YouTube**
If you have difficulties writing a great business vision statement watch this 5-minute video from Dr Susan L. Reid, **How-to Write a Great Business Vision Statement,**
https://www.youtube.com/watch?v=Jtz05G1B4i8

(3)

Do
Writing down and understanding your own vision statement will provide clarity and direction not only to you the entrepreneur but also to your stakeholders and employees. Good vision statements often have common components:

- It is written in the present, not future tense. ...
- It is summarised with a powerful phrase. ...
- It describes an outcome; the best outcome we can achieve. ...
- It uses unequivocal language. ...
- It evokes emotion. ...
- It helps build a picture, the same picture, in people's minds.

Use the above guide and construct your own vision statement.

Vision:
_____
_____
_____
_____

5 - Point plan

Understanding the values derived from a well-defined vision will assist you in understanding the importance of a well-defined vision:

- It supports the entrepreneurs understanding and expectation of potential opposition.
- It is a clear indication of what the aspirations are with regards to a future state.
- It clarifies what is in scope of an organisation's business activities and exclude what is out of scope.
- It is an indication to stakeholders and shareholders of the drive and aspirations of the organisation or of the entrepreneurs.
- It assists with the allocation of resources and is a clear indication to markets of the organisations drivers.

Read

12 Truly Inspiring Company Vision and Mission Statement Examples, By Lindsay Kolowich,
https://blog.hubspot.com/marketing/inspiring-company-mission-statements#sm.0001772c5ke6tcymw6s14mzfaqv3x

(3B)

2.2 Mission

"The business mission is so rarely given adequate thought it is perhaps the most important single cause of business frustration"
Peter Drucker

You might ask what is the difference between an organisation's vision and mission statements. We have already spoken about vision as clarifying the future and that mission statements describe the present. A mission statement intends clarifying the 'what' and 'who' of a company. Mission statements should be communicating the essence of your business to your stakeholders, customers and to the public at large. Why do you exist as a business, what is your goals, who are your customers, how do you meet customer needs, how do you differ from competitors etc.?

Examples of some corporate mission statements:
The Bank of New York - The Bank of New York is a financial institution geared towards traditional banking, insurance, and investment services. With over 350 branches, the Bank of New York specializes in securities servicing, treasury management and investment management in order to aid enterprises manage their finances more effectively.

Mission Statement: We strive to be the acknowledged global leader and preferred partner in helping our clients succeed in the world's rapidly evolving financial markets.

Chevron - Chevron is a global energy and oil company whose headquarters are in San Ramon, California. Aside from offering oil and natural gas, Chevron also develops hydrogen infrastructure, advanced battery systems, Nano-materials and renewable energy applications.

Mission Statement: At the heart of The Chevron Way is our Vision to be the global energy company most admired for its people, partnership and performance.

Ford Motor Company - The instigator of the manufacturing revolution of mass production assembly lines, the Ford Motor Company is one of the largest manufacturers of transportation vehicles, particularly cars and trucks. The cars they manufactured include Ford, Lincoln, Mercury, Mazda, Volvo, Jaguar, Land Rover, and Aston Martin.

Mission Statement: We are a global family with a proud heritage passionately committed to providing personal mobility for people around the world.

Debate

Review your current position, understand if you are content for it to remain as it is or do you or your organisation have a desire to develop a new and / or existing meaningful mission statement?

If you are ready for change or don't have a mission statement, think about what needs to be done to create a mission statement? Discuss your current or suggest a mission statement with your employees, stakeholders and customers. Start developing your own mission statement by answering the "what" and "how" questions of your business.

Watch: How to Write a Mission Statement – YouTube

If you need some inspiration to write your mission statements watch this short 5-minute video by Erica Olsen, **How to Write a Mission Statement,** *https://www.youtube.com/watch?v=XtyCt83JLNY*

(4)

Do

Writing down and understanding your own mission statement will provide clarity and direction not only to you the entrepreneur but also to your stakeholders and employees. Good mission statements often provide answers to the following questions:

- **Customers:** Who are your customers?
- **Products and services:** What are your product and service offerings?
- **Markets:** Where do you compete?
- **Technology:** What is your basic technology?
- **Concern for survival, growth, and profitability:** What is your commitment towards economic objectives?
- **Philosophy:** What are your basic beliefs, core values, aspirations and philosophical priorities?
- **Self-concept:** What are your strengths and competitive advantages?
- **Concern for public image:** What is your business' public image?
- **Concern for employees:** What is your business attitude or orientation towards employees?

Use the above guide and construct your own mission statement.

Mission:
_____
_____
_____
_____

---

5 - Point plan

Before constructing your mission statement, consider the following:
- Mission statements help businesses to identify its essential business.
- Mission statements act as a road map for businesses.

- Mission statements make it possible for businesses to make an effective difference.
- Mission statements provide a powerful tool for business leaders and entrepreneurs.
- Mission statements provide "identity" to a business.

Read

Read and enjoy an article written by **Nicole Fallon, What is a Mission Statement?** *https://www.businessnewsdaily.com/3783-mission-statement.html*

(5)

2.3 Clarify objectives

"Objectives can be compared to a compass bearing by which a ship navigates. A compass bearing is firm, but "in actual navigation, a ship may veer off its course for many miles. Without a compass bearing, a ship would neither find its port nor be able to estimate the time required to get there"
Peter Drucker

Many of us are challenged with setting objectives and then chasing what we believe is a noble cause? Some of us also have to achieve objectives set by others.

This makes the road difficult and gives us a good reason to criticise the expectation as it is someone else's dream normally set without understanding what it will take to achieve or being unrealistic. In order to move forward we need to create an understanding of what an objective is, what is the purpose of objectives, how to set objectives, how to evaluate objectives and how to achieve objectives.

When looking at objectives it could be personal or business orientated. In short setting objectives should move us to action. The best way to go about setting objectives is to align it with the company vision and mission. Objective could be short-term, 12 to 24 months or longer-term, normally 5 years' maximum. Setting objectives is typically the responsibility of management or for start-ups that of the business owner. Setting of objectives should not be set in isolation, it is important to involve all stakeholders that will be involved in the execution of the objective. Objectives should preferably meet the SMART principal:

S = Specific – What needs to be done and by whom?
Increase sales per sales representative in the spares division by 10% per month using the January 2016 sales as the base information to make the projection.

M = Measurable – How will it be measured for example; Increase sales revenue from R100 k per month to R110 k per month

A = Attainable – Although objectives needs to be a stretch from the current position it also needs to be attainable. Setting objectives that are clearly unattainable are a waste of time, energy and resources. You might also battle to get buy-in from sales and other departments if the set objectives are perceived to be unattainable.

R – Realistic and Timely – Realistic objectives are those that could be attained within the period allocated and are timely, given the phase of execution in which the organisation finds itself. Being timely could also relate to seasonality as it is pointless for example to set a target for an increase in Christmas tree sales in March of each year as its clearly out of season unless its supported with an out of season promotion to stimulate early purchases.

Company and or marketing objectives needs to be set because of a clear understanding of any company growth or sustainable agenda as setting objectives are pointless if it's not properly resourced.

Constantly ask yourself in order to deliver on the set objectives – what is needed and what resources are required? Once the objectives are set by the entrepreneur or management it needs to be communicated to the rest of the organisation. Objectives are such a critical part to the successful implementation of any strategy that if it is not clearly communicated it will not be achieved. The setting of poor and weak objectives will lead to the achievement of poor and weak results. Every individual in a company needs to know and understand what their duties and responsibilities are in the execution of the set objectives. Not only will the setting of meaningful and thoughtful objectives provide focus to an organisation's activities, but it will also assist management and individuals to track progress and take corrective actions timeously.

Care should be taken with the setting of objectives, as it is not a tactical activity and should preferably not be changed during the time frame allocated for achievement. Business and marketing strategies should have a combination of primary and secondary objectives. Primary objectives are captured in the framework structure of a marketing plan (objectives that the plan needs to deliver) with market strategies such as product, competitor and brand strategies reflecting secondary objectives. Objectives are not set in stone but should support one another and be in line with the business plan. Objectives should be supportive and compatible with the organisations values. Objectives are often perceived as actions to turn dreams into reality.

> *"The difference between goals and mission is reflected in the difference between I want to get married and I want to have a successful marriage"*
> **Author Unknown**

Example of a good business objective - Focus Areas: Financial Growth, Customer Satisfaction, Innovation, Product Growth, People, Culture, Processes and Operations:
- Reduce production overheads by 10% by the end of quarter 3, 2021.
- Increase customer satisfaction by 15 points by 2020.

- Launch three new products by 31st Dec 2019.
- Establish four new major distribution partnerships by 1st Feb 2025.
- Reduce staff nutrition to less than 10% per annum by 1st Jan 2026.
- Lose fewer than two major accounts per year until 1st Dec 2019.
- Hire five additional product managers by 1st Feb 2017.
- Reduce product return rate to less than 2% by 1st Jan 2018.

Also see below an example of a more general business objective set by the Coca-Cola Company "…..To be globally known as a business that conducts business responsibly and ethically and to accelerate sustainable growth to operate in tomorrow's world". By having these type of objectives, it forms the foundation for companies in the decision making process.

Debate

Setting your personal and business objectives will provide clarity and direction not only to you the entrepreneur but also to your stakeholders and employees. Good objectives will be supportive of your vision and mission statements. If you already have personal and business objectives set, debate whether they are still relevant and contributing to your vision and mission statements. Avoid having to many objectives as it just confuses activities and are often difficult to measure.

If you do not have objectives formulised and are still in the developmental phase set your objectives, and debate it with team members, peers and selected customer. This might give you some additional insights and even shape your objectives into double actions.

Watch: 🎥 Setting Objectives - Video 1 and 2 – YouTube

If you need some inspiration to formulate and to write your personal and or business objectives watch this short 3-minute video by David Bozward, **Setting Objectives,**
https://www.youtube.com/watch?v=hD9gaqZ94UQ

(6)

Watch this 16-minute video by Geoff Riley, for setting more specific business objectives
https://www.youtube.com/watch?v=KxjbQ3otNIE

(7)

Do 👆

Writing down your personal and business objectives is the first step in formulating your actions and drivers for the future. Objectives are a view of expectations in the future, an indication of the desired state. Once the objectives have been formulated and noted it tends to take on a form of reality and no longer is it something that could be ignored. As a follow-up on the broad goals set in Chapter 1 let us build on those and consider some additional criteria in evaluating your objectives.

	Evaluating Criteria	Objective 1	Objective 2	Objective 3
1	Is my objective measurable?			
2	Is my objective broad?			
3	Could I assign a person to be responsible for this area of activity?			
4	Is my objective continuous, ongoing, and non-dated?			
5	Does my objective convert my vision and mission into action?			
6	Does my objective help to sustain my competitive advantage?			

5 - Point plan

Setting personal and business objectives will be one of the most important elements of your plan, take care that it includes the following elements:

- Specific – Be very specific to eliminate any grey areas.
- Stale – Objectives without a time period and due date is meaningless.
- Realistic – Objectives must be a stretch but also realistic.
- Focused on the shorter-term – Starting of short term objectives are important as it could evolve in longer-term objectives, but start at the beginning.
- Open to adjustments as needed – Objectives are definitive, but should be open to adjustment by the objective holder.

Read

Read and enjoy an article written by George N Root III, **10 Most Important Business Objectives,**
http://smallbusiness.chron.com/10-important-business-objectives-23686.html

(8)

2.3.1 Barriers to achieving business plan objectives

"The result of bad communication is a disconnection between strategy and execution."
Chuck Martin, former vice president, IBM

Some of the most common barriers to the achievement of objectives start with the continuous change in strategy and direction. Entrepreneurs must guard against jumping from opportunity to opportunity without reflecting on its influence on the execution of existing objectives.

Objectives set without prioritisation and support by senior management will not be effective, as it will be perceived as less important. Entrepreneurs setting business objectives without resourcing organisations to enable implementation will fail in delivering on the set objectives. Unclear expectations concerning the outcome or net benefit of achieving the objective could lead to weak measurement and disappointment with the end result. Poor communication from management to workers could lead to poor implementation of objectives and workers not being sure of what are expected of them.

Businesses should set objectives as part of business and marketing plans to ensure sustainability and continuous business growth. Operating a business without a business plan and set objectives is like driving a car without a steering wheel.

> *"What you get by achieving your goals is not as important as what you become by achieving your goals"*
> **Zig Ziglar (1926 -) Motivational Speaker and Author**

Debate

Executing any strategy or delivering on set objectives are often difficult and many reasons could be provided for a lack of performance. As an entrepreneur or business manager consider and debate the following as possible barriers to the successful implementation of your business plan and objectives: How relevant are these barriers to your success?

- Organisational divides or silos that often leads to a lack of cooperation.
- A lack of detailed information linking objectives to benefits and actions.
- Management and leaders in the organisation are not committed to the set objectives and does not support it.
- Poor planning processes and poor planning of what is required to implement the plans and objectives.
- Outdated systems and technology, not allowing the organisation to move forward with the implementation of planned objectives.

Watch: Overcome Obstacles and Challenges to Achieve a Goal - YouTube

Overcoming barriers to achieve objectives and more specific business plan objectives. Watch this short 5-minute video by Stephen Goldberg **Overcome Obstacles and Challenges to Achieve a Goal,**
https://www.youtube.com/watch?v=uuWhqzJLFF8

(9)

Do
One way to overcome obstacles or barriers in the successful implementation and execution of business plan objectives would be to first being able to correctly identify the obstacles and then formulate mitigation actions to overcome these obstacles. Use the table below with your team members or business partners to identify potential obstacles and to workshop potential mitigation actions.

Objectives	Obstacles	Who is responsible to deliver on the objectives?	What are the consequences of not delivering on the objectives?	Mitigation Plan to achieve objectives
1.				
2.				
3.				
4.				

5 Point plan
As indicated before we could debate many reasons why we fail to deliver on set objectives but as entrepreneurs and business people, we must avoid some of the basic barriers to the successful implementation of business objectives such as:
- Being narrow minded.
- Poor focus or direction and having a lack of experience.
- Inability to identify and take opportunities.
- Fear of failure, fear of success and fear of rejection.
- Having limited resources and inadequate support.

Read

Read and enjoy an article written by Kay Fudala, **How to Overcome Barriers To Achieving Goals,**
http://redgramliving.com/2013/08/20/how-to-overcome-barriers-to-achieving-goals/

(10)

"When defeat comes, accept it as a signal that your plans are not sound, rebuild those plans, and set sail once more toward your coveted goal."
Napoleon Hill

So What's your Plan?

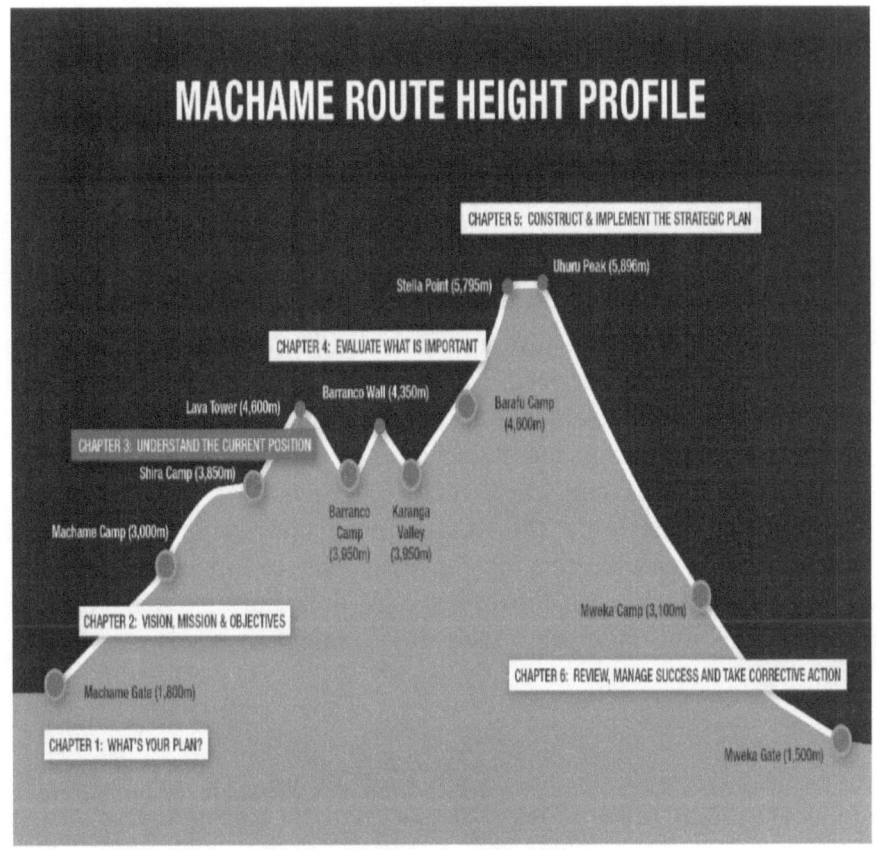

Personal Camp – Journey: Shira Barranco Camp
Day 3 on mountain
Shira camp – Barranco Camp 3,847m (12,621ft) – 3,985m (13,071ft)
Average hiking time: 7 hours
A morning of gentle ascent and panoramic views, leaving the moorland plateau behind to walk on lava ridges beneath the glaciers of the Western Breach. After lunch near the Lava Tower junction (4,500m) we descend to the bottom of the Great Barranco Valley, sheltered by towering cliffs with extensive views of the plains far below. **Overnight at Barranco Camp**

Chapter 3: Understand the current position

"It is not the strongest of the species that survive, nor the most intelligent, but the one most responsive to change"
Charles Darwin

We can only hope to get a better understanding of our current position by scanning our environment and bring some context to our position relevant to the rest of the world we find ourselves in or within we plan to participate. Most people do not bother much with this very important element of moving from one given state to a desire state resulting in inevitable failure. How many entrepreneurs have lost their lifesavings in a venture because they have not made the time to understand the environment that they will have to function in? Most investors also have an issue to support or invest in other people's dreams if those that seek financial or other forms of support does not understand their environment themselves – would you?

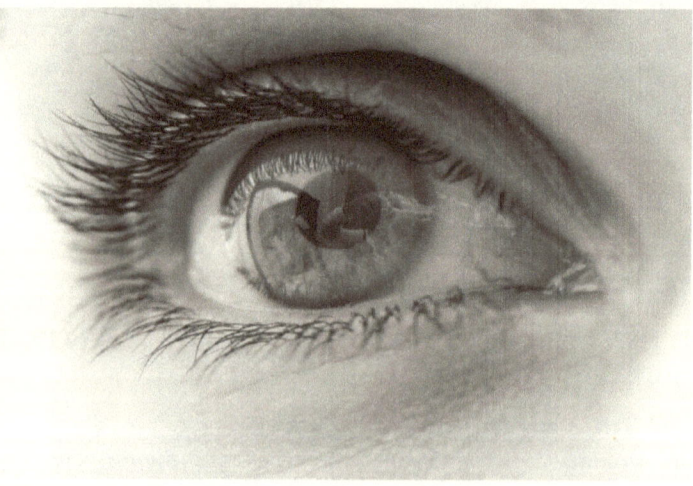

Business scanning is a process used to observe and record activities in the external and internal environments with the intention to better understand these environments and to assist in decision making about threats and opportunities.

There are several methods that could be used for this process from common-sense to more formal activities such as the macro and micro market, customers, competitors, suppliers and swot analysis. Following the clarification of the business Vision, Mission and Objectives is the process of business scanning.

Debate

Debate with team members when last you or your organisation have conducted a business scanning process to observe and record activities in the internal and external environments with the intention to better understand these environments and to assist in decision making within your organisation? Have you been able to position your business or organisation relevant to the environment? Being able to respond fast to changing environments provide organisations with a competitive advantage. Do you or your management team understand the value of environmental scanning? What benefits do you foresee from observing and record activities in the internal and external environments?

Watch: Environmental scanning - YouTube

Watch this short 4.5-minute video by Teo Hiro, **How Internal and External Factors Drive Organizational Change** to obtain a better understanding of environmental scanning and its benefits to an organisation, *https://www.youtube.com/watch?v=Kt6J-jCcdXk*

(11)

Do

Before embarking on a full-scale environmental analysis, evaluate your current status and understanding of the following factors and its influences on your current or potential business activities:

Some examples of internal environmental factors for consideration					
	Understanding within business			Influences on business	
	Low	Medium	High	Low	High
Management changes					
Employee morale					
Culture changes					
Financial changes and/or issues					

Some examples of external environmental factors for consideration					
	Understanding within business			Influences on business	
	Low	Medium	High	Low	High
Changes to the economy					
Threats from competitors					
Political factors					
Government regulations					
The industry itself					

The above is by no means a complete list of factors or elements for consideration when evaluating your current level of environmental scanning but it will get you thinking of the importance of updated data and information obtained from regular scanning.

5 - Point plan

An environmental scan is an assessment and analysis of the conditions, circumstances and influences, both internal and external to the organisation, which may affect the organisation's ability to achieve its objectives, however before starting the process you need to make a few decisions regarding the process and methods you will follow during the scanning process:

- What types of environmental scanning will you use?
- What process of environmental scanning do you plan to follow?

- What techniques and or methods of environmental scanning will best suite your needs?
- What is the importance of environmental scanning for you and your organisation?
- What advantages will the process of environmental analysis bring to you or your organisation?

Read

Read and enjoy an article written by Vibhav Srivastava, **Importance of Understanding Business Environment,**
http://in.viadeo.com/en/groups/detaildiscussion/?containerId=0021 t7mup2amy1o5&forumId=00218vlbvywso7e3&action=messageDet ail&messageId=0025811ykdrvs0y

(12)

Entrepreneurs and business managers need to understand that the creator of the business and or marketing plan is the owner of the plan and the implementation thereof and therefore need to do some homework with regards to the critical elements of a plan. One such element will be the external (Macro) business environment.

3.1 Macro environmental analysis (external)

"The opportunities and threats existing in any situation always exceed the resources needed to exploit the opportunities or avoid the threat. Thus, strategy is essentially a problem of allocating resources. If strategy is to be successful, it must allocate superior resources against a decisive opportunity"
William Cohen

The Macro environment refers to all the elements that exist outside a company, but that have an influence on a company's performance. These elements such as economy, government policies, technology, legal, social conditions and nature to name but a few are outside the control of a company or an individual. Not understanding them or being ignorant of its existence and the impact of these elements on a company's ability to be competitive could be disastrous and would not assist in attracting investors.

Entrepreneurs, marketing and sales people hoping to establish new business ventures or gain new customers need to review the elements relevant to its industry or situation. The success of an organisation to survive consists of two dimensions: its ability to scan and analyse the environment at a macro and micro level, but most important to respond timeously in an appropriate manner to capitalise on the constant changing environments.

Debate

Debate internally in your team or with customers your understanding of the external environment and your level of understanding of this environment. Consider when last, if at all, you reviewed the changes in the macro environment. What would the benefits be if your organisation scanned the macro environment on a more regular basis? What would the cost be to conduct a formal scanning project and what competitive advantage could be gained from this activity. Do you have the resources to scan the macro environment or would you have to make use of external resources? Does the organisation have a culture to respond with speed to changes in the environment? What would the cost be of not doing a macro (external) analysis?

Watch: Macro Environmental Forces - YouTube
Watch this short 4.5-minute video by Art Mollengarden, **Macro Environmental Forces**,
https://www.youtube.com/watch?v=lgzeSkil1SE

(13)

Do

As an individual, entrepreneur planning to establish a new business or acting as a business leader within a larger team ask yourself; "Are you aware of the external forces that could have an influence on your business success, and if yes, when last have you reviewed them and what was your response to these forces?" Use the table below to do a quick assessment:

External Environment	Awareness Yes / No	Last Review date	Response to influence, mitigation
Economy			
Government Policy's			
Technology			
Legal			
Social and Cultural Conditions			
Nature (Environmental)			

2 - Point plan

As entrepreneurs and business leaders, we need to constantly be aware of changes in our external environment and be able to pre-empt some of these changes and have mitigations in place to manage or capitalise on these ever changing forces. With the external environment being divided into two parts ensure you understand the short term and long-term impact of these forces:

- **Directly interactive:** This environment has an immediate and first hand impact upon the organisation. A new competitor entering the market is an example. This might require urgent action from entrepreneurs or business leaders.
- **Indirectly interactive:** This environment has a secondary and more distant effect upon the organisation. New legislation taking effect may have a great impact. For example, complying with the new Consumer Act requires organisations to display the country of origin on product packaging. Organisations might have longer lead times to respond to these requirements and should be plan for it accordingly. Understanding the urgency will allow you to plan and respond accordingly with specific focus on resource allocation.

Read

Read and enjoy an article written by Jim Tischler, **Macro environmental Forces Affecting Marketing,**
http://smallbusiness.chron.com/macroenvironmental-forces-affecting-marketing-71632.html

(14)

Reviewing some of the following elements would be beneficial in building an understanding of the macro environment for most organisations.

3.1.1 Economy - Things to consider

"Economy is too late when you are at the bottom of your purse"
Seneca (4 BC-65) Roman philosopher and playwright.

Some of the more simplistic economic factors affecting business include consumer confidence, employment, interest rates and inflation. Entrepreneurship tends to focus on identifying and fulfilling consumer needs in selected markets, but all businesses can be affected by large-scale economic trends. Accounting for trends in the overall economy can help entrepreneurs and business leaders make better decisions.

The economy refers to income, expenditure and resources that affect the cost of operating a business or a household. Before starting a new business or even assessing potential growth areas, you need to follow economic trends and future happenings likely to have influences on the economy. Entrepreneurs need to take decisions and position activities to counter constrained economic environments or decide to capitalise on good economic growth by investing in opportunities of infrastructure to support growth initiatives. It's often difficult to predict what to do and where to influence to be ahead of the game or just to survive in changing economic situations, but having a better understanding of the current and potential future status will assist you with making more informed decisions.

Debate

In order to improve your understanding of the economic environment and its influence on your current and future business, discuss your level of insight with team members and compile a list of economic issues that is of concern. This list of concerns could also be registered as business risks that need to be managed. This list could potentially lead to the exploration of opportunities and support investment decisions. It is important that you assess your position on a regular basis.

Watch: How to review business economic factors – YouTube

Watch this short 4.5-minute video by Terry Rachwalski, **How to review business economic factors,** *https://www.youtube.com/watch?v=mz5D7FFGptM*

(15)

Do

Evaluate your understanding of the economic environment by exploring answers to the following questions relevant to your current business or future business opportunities:

- What is the current state of the economy in the area or within the country, you would like to operate?
- What is the effected GDP (Gross Domestic Product) rate or the inflation rate?
- How does this influence consumer spend?
- What the historical trends are with regards to the interest rates and investments?
- What are the income patterns of the consumers in the market you are targeting?
- Do customers or consumers have disposable income or is there a general feeling of recession?
- What is the consumer's gross income?
- What is the consumer's discretionary income?
- Which customers or areas do you target – are they part of the general population or less influenced by the trends of the economic climate?
- Would customers buy your products or services under the current economic climate?
- What is the prospect for the economy over the short and long term?

- Would banks be willing to support start-up companies or are they more interested in supporting the expansion programs of existing companies?

5 - Point plan

If you are an entrepreneur or small business manager and are unsure where to start and what to focus on to assist you to be better informed about the economy and its effect on your business, it is suggested that you focus on the following elements to give you a basic understanding:
- What is the state of the economic growth normally expressed as a percentage?
- What are the current and projected inflation rate as well as interest rate?
- What is the current and projected employment rate?
- What government policies have changed or are about to change that might affect your business?
- What is the state of the global economy and what effect will change in the global economy have on your business?

Read

Read and enjoy an article written by Anders Borg, **6-Factors shaping the global economy in 2016,**
https://www.weforum.org/agenda/.../6-factors-shaping-the-global-economy-in-2016/

(16)

3.1.2 Government Policy - Things to consider

Governments create the rules and frameworks in which businesses are able to compete against each other. From time to time, the government will change these rules and frameworks forcing businesses to change the way they operate. Government policy's may differ from country to country and may even vary from favourable, to reasonable to ridiculous.

However, entrepreneurs globally need to understand the policies and expectations from its local government to survive in an ever changing world. For example: Some local government might offer support to small and medium size organisations and if your organisation fit the definition, why not make use of the support? On the other hand, if your local government makes it difficult for small businesses to establish manufacturing facilities then you might have to decide to buy from other suppliers or to import to avoid local manufacturing taxes. Whatever the government policies are in specific geographical areas both entrepreneurs starting off or with already established businesses would need to ensure they constantly updated with regards to changes in policy. If you know about changes or can anticipate some changes will come about it will assist you to make better decisions to capitalise on the changes or to avoid additional burdens.

Changes in government policies are often published via a Government Gazette, however lobbying for changes in policy takes place at many levels and entrepreneurs could influence the outcome and changes of policy through inputs at local government and trade bodies. Policymaking is the process of changing an idea into an action. These 'ideas' can come from many different places, for example:
- Government
- Ministers
- Politicians
- Councillors
- Civil servants
- Society
- Voluntary organisations

- Community groups
- Trade unions
- Professionals, such as doctors and academics
- Public opinion
- People like you

The list of people involved in shaping policy ideas is almost endless, but unless you start taking part, your views will never make a difference. Staying ahead of the game is influencing policy and remaining informed!

Debate

Debate with your team members or partners your level of understanding of local governments policy influences on your organisation or potential growth initiatives. If you are already in operation, when last have you reviewed the influence of these policies on your business and which new obligations have been placed on your business? Most individual entrepreneurs follow changes in policies and try to capitalise on the favourable changes to the benefit of the organisation, but often neglect to plan for the mitigation of addition risk by not complying with changes in policy. Sometimes this could be intentional but mostly it is because if ignorance, which could be a costly mistake.

Watch: Main influences: Government policies | Business Studies - YouTube

Watch this short 2.5-minute video by Moira Millard, **Main influences: Government policies | Business Studies,** *https://www.youtube.com/watch?v=lTx9Z5rDYUQ*

(17)

Do

The role of government and government policies on the competitiveness of companies should not be under estimated. If your competitors are better at understanding the influences of the changes in policy and are better placed to capitalise from these changes then they will have a competitive advantage over your efforts. Ask yourself a few simple questions:

- What is the view of government, concerning entrepreneurs starting a new venture and what level of support do they provide?
- Does government allow free trade and protect smaller entities?
- Does government support a new venture or the development of a new market by legislating policies that will support development in selected areas?
- What support does government supply? Some governments support entrepreneurs with training, start-up capital and many other development programmes.
- What tax relief does government allow for small and medium size organisations?
- Does government allow tax incentives for employment creation?
- What is the influence of the changes in the minimum wage in your organisation?
- What is the government policy, concerning imports and exports?
- What is the government policy, concerning local manufacturing and local content?

5 - Point plan

Not keeping abreast of local government policy's and changes will place your new venture or established business at risk worst of all you might be missing out on opportunities? Consider the following to improve your position:

- Keep a simple record of government policies related to your business and the communities in which you conduct business in.
- Make sure you understand the local policies applicable to your business.
- Seek opportunities to lobby for changes to these policies to better your position and improve your competiveness.
- If others are not compliant to these policies but you are, make sure your customers are aware of your compliance as this could assist you to obtain a premium for your products and or services.
- Seek opportunities to capitalise from changes in government policies.

Read

Read and enjoy an article written by Joynal Abdin, **Impact of government policies on business,**
https://www.linkedin.com/pulse/impact-government-policies-business-md-joynal-abdin

(18)

3.1.3 Technology - Things to consider

"If we continue to develop our technology without wisdom or prudence, our servant may prove to be our executioner"
Omar Bradley (General, US Army)

Technology advances are normally because of applied research and could be very unpredictable. Improvements in technology could be applied as a competitive advantage or could seriously hamper the competitive capabilities of an organisation.

Entrepreneurs need to be aware of changes or improvements regarding technology in order to remain competitive. Technology results in change, and businesses that do not adapt to these changes swiftly are consumed by them. Agility can be a tremendous asset to companies in this rapidly evolving technological age. However, the organisations that compete the best in an ever-changing technological environment are those who have the foresight to stay ahead of the curve.

Debate

Explore your current level of understanding of the influence of technological advances on your business or identified opportunities with team members and industry leaders. Debate the answers to the questions below:

- What is the potential influence of technological advances in the industry you are focusing on or the activity you plan to explore?
- What influence does it have on prices, quality and relationships?
- What new products will be developed and how would that influence your offering or objectives?
- Could you be part of the technological developments or would you be a victim?
- Consider the developments of the internet, the World Wide Web and the impact on-line commercial services might have on your proposed business or targeted initiative?
- Could you bring new technologies to the market?
- What is the governments support for new technology developments?

Watch: Back to The Future - Technology and the Four Big Trends that will impact the next 15 years - YouTube

Watch this interesting 16:30-minute video by Daniel Priestley, **Back To The Future - Technology and the Four Big Trends that will impact the next 15 years,**
https://www.youtube.com/watch?v=yEZcsgA4JsQ

(19)

Do

Not investing in new technology or understanding the impact of technological advancements on your business could be risky as it could put you out of business, however before you decide what route to take consider the following:

- Organisational change, what changes does the organisation need to go through to implement the new technologies'? Or what organisational changes need to take place to remain competitive in a changing technological environment?
- Which? changes in business processes need to be supported or developed to remain competitive in an ever changing technological environment?
- What would the adoption or rejection of technological advances have on your organisations sustainable competitive advantage?
- What would the costs be to introduce new technologies or the cost of not keeping up with the changes in technological improvements?
- Which benefits would the technological improvements have on your organisations efficiency and or productivity?

5 - Point plan

Some entrepreneurs lead the race on technological advancements and other follow, however before embarking on internal developments or evaluating alternative offers, consider the following benefits associated with advances in technology, and the opportunities it can create for your business:
- Reduction in business costs and the ability to compete with other larger organisations on an equal footing?
- Improvement in communication processes.
- Improvement in your employee productivity using advance technology?
- Advancements in technology's assistance to reach new markets?
- Advances in technology assist organisations with the ability to outsource functions to the cheapest areas possible, including foreign countries?

Read

Read and enjoy an article written by Alex Pirouz, **The Impact of Technology in Business,**
www.businessreviewaustralia.com/technology/.../The-Impact-of-Technology-in-Busin.

(20)

3.1.4 Legal – Things to consider

"The law is reason, free from passion"
Aristotle (384 BC-322 BC) Greek philosopher.

Legal restrictions or support refers to the laws that govern activities in a country or in an industry. Legal compliance is critical to ethical organisations and entrepreneurs in exploring any new opportunity business need to be aware of legal requirements that could positively or negatively influence its success.

Many examples of changes in legislation such as the implementation of the Consumer Protection Act, 2008 (Act No.68 of 2008) had profound influences on business activities. Both new start-ups and established businesses had to comply with the new Act. In some instances, businesses influenced the establishment of the act and benefited from the new legislation as they pre-empted the changes and were well positioned to capitalise on the changes. Others were court unaware of the changes and were ill prepared to cope with the changes resulting in an increase in risk and an increase in cost to meet compliance. Non-compliance to changing legislation could lead to business closure and lost opportunities. Entrepreneurs and business leaders need to take care of all legal requirements when managing a business or evaluating new opportunities to avoid disappointment.

It is also important in your planning process to understand competitor compliance levels with legislation as low levels of compliance or no compliance by competitors could provide your business with a competitive advantage, one that needs to be highlighted to customers and authorities.

Debate

As a responsible entrepreneur, business owner and leader you have an obligation to ensure you operate within the ruling legislation and keep abreast of any changes that might affect your business or future opportunities. Debate the answers to the questions below with your team members or legal representatives to ensure you are ahead of the game and are able to identify any areas to convert into opportunities to outsmart competitors.

- What are the laws for new entrances to a market, industry or country?
- What are the competition laws applicable to your industry?
- What is the product or service laws that you are expected to comply with?
- What are the company laws and tax laws applicable to your venture or business?
- What protection do you have under the patent laws and copyright laws?
- Which laws exist to protect your consumers from abuse that you need to comply with?
- What pricing or distribution laws are in place to protect both yourself and consumers that you need to adhere to or take advantage off?
- Which advertising or promotion legislation exists that you need to comply with?

Watch: 5 Legal Basics Entrepreneurs Need to Know - YouTube

Watch this interesting 16:30-minute video by Merissa V Grayson , **5 Legal Basics Entrepreneurs Need to Know,**
https://www.youtube.com/watch?v=TpEwgbgzeMc

(21)

Do

Businesses, small or large are continuously operating in environments governed by legislation that evolve over time. The way in which a business can operate and function is controlled by legislation. Global and local authorities can impose laws.

Legislation mainly acts as a constraint on business. It is important that entrepreneurs or business leaders understand and are aware of the legislation they need to comply with and understand the risks of non-compliance. The main areas of legislation that affects businesses are below (evaluate your level of compliance and risk exposure):

Legislation	Level of compliance			Risk exposure	
	Low	Medium	High	Low	High
Employment law					
Consumer protection					
Competition law					

5 - Point plan

Taking steps to meet your legal obligations might seem like a management no-brainer, but only fulfilling your minimum requirements might result in missed opportunities. Understanding the reasons for the various rules, laws and regulations that govern your business will help you take advantage of any benefits they offer. Consider the following benefits of compliance:

- It reduces organisational and individual risk.
- It drives efficiencies and economies of scale.
- It levels the playing field, small, medium and large businesses are all the same under the law and needs to comply.
- It enhances relationships with regulators and other stakeholders.
- Helps attract and retain talent and ensure employee engagement.

Read

Read and enjoy an article written by Chad Brooks, **9 Regulatory Issues That Will Affect Small Business's**,
http://www.businessnewsdaily.com/5673-small-business-laws-in2014.html#sthash.uabzKbfD.dpuf

(22)

3.1.5 Social and Cultural Conditions – Things to consider

"The soul takes nothing with her to the next world but her education and her culture. At the beginning of the journey to the next world, one's education and culture can either provide the greatest assistance, or else act as the greatest burden, to the person who has just died"
Plato, the Republic of Plato

Being in business is not only about knowing how to make sales and generate great profits, but it also involves understanding the environment you are operating in. Social-cultural factors are the lifestyle of a group of people, their customs and their value system. Religion predominantly influenced the social-cultural factors of a group of people.

Other factors are their language, the law of their land, politics and the economic status of the people. Social-cultural behaviour of society's markets segments also indicates to entrepreneurs and business leaders what the current or potential trends and behaviours could be in a market. Some organisations have ignored these social and cultural behavioural changes and as a result made costly mistakes that are difficult to recover from.

Debate

Debate your understanding of some of the questions below relating to social and cultural factors that drive your market and customers that will assist in a better understanding of how to market your products and services to these communities. The questions below are just a start and many more could be debated, avoid being ignorant to these social and cultural behaviours as communities will reject your advances and sometimes even consider your organisation as being disrespectful.

- What are their values, attitudes and ideas?
- What is their view on the changing role of a woman?
- What is the make-up of the population you are targeting?
- Size of the population, gender and potential age groups?
- Which generation do they represent "baby boomers" generation X etc.?
- Are they working, retired or students?
- Do they live in the cities or out of town?
- Married or unmarried?
- What lifestyle do they enjoy?
- Which consumer attitude and options do they express?
- What is their current standard of living or what do they aspire to?
- What are their needs regarding to education and social liberties?

Watch: The Social Environment and Cultural Environment – YouTube

Watch this short 5:54 minutes video by Alanis Business Academy, **The Social Environment,**
https://www.youtube.com/watch?v=rXty8_fMjk4

(23)

Also watch this short 2:17-minute video by B2Bwhiteboard, **Cultural Environment,**
https://www.youtube.com/watch?v=2M0GDRhS0MA

(24)

Do

Entrepreneurs need to be aware of the social and cultural situations and trends of the communities and target market they plan to operate in and act accordingly. If you are already servicing communities or plan to exploit an opportunity, consider your level of understanding of the proposed social and cultural influences below; are you aware of these influences? Are you sensitive to them and from a business point of view do you have a plan in place to capitalise from these behaviours?

Social and Cultural behaviours	Aware of the influence		Are you sensitive to this influence		Do you have a plan in place to capitalise from these behaviours	
	Yes	No	Yes	No	Yes	No
Communication with selected group / target market						
Level of purchasing power						
Religious days						
Advertising selection methods						
Family arrangements						

Social and Cultural behaviours	Aware of the influence		Are you sensitive to this influence		Do you have a plan in place to capitalise from these behaviours	
	Yes	No	Yes	No	Yes	No
Religious practices						
Local laws						
Some local believes						
Level of education						
Social structure or levels of authority						

2 - Point plan

Entrepreneurs and business leaders hoping to influence selected target markets needs to have a good understanding of socio - cultural factors unique to the selected markets if they seek action from these particular groups. Consider the following in your interpretation of your selected markets socio - cultural factors:

- Cultural aspects include concepts of beauty, education, language, law and politics, religion, social organisations, technology and material culture, values and attitudes.
- Social factors include reference groups, family, role and status in society, time and available resources.

Read

Read and enjoy an article written by Joseph Zammit-Lucia, **Businesses cannot avoid involvement in cultural, social and moral issues,**
https://www.theguardian.com/sustainable-business/business-confront-cultural-social-moral-issues

(25)

3.1.6 Nature (Environmental) – Things to consider

"Earth provides enough to satisfy every man's needs, but not every man's greed"
Mahatma Gandhi

Nature or the environment around us as individuals or business has a definitive influence on our long-term survival as individuals or sustainability as organisations. Entrepreneurs who select to ignore a business' influence on the environment and its consequential influence on consumer behaviour risk the long-term sustainability of business ventures and could face customer resistance. Besides doing the right thing as a good entrepreneurial or corporate citizen, modern-day society demand from businesses to be responsible in their behaviours to minimise the effect on the environment and in fact demand from businesses to display their behaviour in this regard. Consumers are generally willing to reward organisations for responsible behaviour with regards to its influence on the environment. It is thus important for entrepreneurs or business leaders to continuously evaluate its impact on the environment and work on systems, processes and innovations to minimise its effect on the environment.

However, to start this process entrepreneurs and business leaders must review their current position and work on scenarios to improve their position going forward in order to build sustainable business models. Claiming innocence or not being aware of business activities affecting the environment will not be tolerated by consumers, legislation and the communities at large.

Debate

Debate with your team members and stakeholders your understanding of some of the environmental challenges you will face as an entrepreneur or organisation, planning to explore new opportunities or to grow existing activities in existing or new geographical areas.

The changes in environmental legislation might also influence what will be expected of new activities going forward. Organisations need to ensure they minimise their impact on the environment to remain relevant and to build long lasting businesses. The questions below will start the internal conversation and highlight the level of responsibilities placed on organisations to limit their impact on the environment. Also, remember that those who have a less harmful impact on the environment will obtain a competitive advantage above competitors.

- If you are to start a manufacturing plant – would it be allowed in the area, you are targeting?
- What is expected of you as an individual or company operating in specific geographical areas?
- What is the impact of your activities on nature in general and would it influence your selected customer purchasing decisions?
- What would your $Co2$ footprint be versus what is acceptable?
- What is the environmental situation in the area or country in which you want to operate?
- What are the weather conditions?

Watch: How Do Business Affect the Environment? – YouTube

Watch this short 1:19-minute video by Coleen Go, **How Do Business Affect the Environment?**
https://www.youtube.com/watch?v=PdgNHVpOsUM

So What's your Plan?

(26)

Do

Business activities affect the local environment - both natural and social. Ethical businesses try to keep the impact of their operations on the environment to a minimum. Consider your current or proposed business activities' social cost on the environment.

Social cost	Influence on the environment			Action plan to address	
	Small	Medium	Large	No	Yes
Noise					
Pollution					
Loss of land					
Congestion					

3 - Point plan

Running an environmentally friendly business helps you reduce your impact on the environment and preserves natural resources. Your business can help the environment in many ways therefore consider the following:

- Use products that reduce your reliance on natural resources (e.g. rainwater tanks, solar hot water systems).
- Use products made from recycled material (e.g. office supplies made from recycled plastic, furniture made from recycled rubber).
- Look at all your business activities to see if you can do anything differently (e.g. reducing air travel by holding conference calls instead of face-to-face meetings).

Making your business environmentally, friendly not only benefits the environment, but can also save you money.

Read

Read and enjoy an article written by Anup Shah, **Corporations and the Environment,**
http://www.globalissues.org/article/55/corporations-and-the-environment

(27)

From the above it is clear that many external elements need to be reviewed and considered in the analysis of the external environment. The above list is by no means comprehensive however would be a minimum consideration for a standard business plan.

Once the elements of the Macro environment are listed, examined and reviewed, it is time to have a closer look at the Micro or internal environment. The Micro environment looks at elements that are within the company or individuals control and are largely in response to the company's adjustments to the Macro environment including its own mission and objectives.

3.2 Micro environmental analysis (internal)

The idea is to concentrate our strength against our competitor's relative weakness
Bruce Henderson

The internal environment also represents many variables influencing a company's competitiveness, market share and position in the community. We will explore some of these elements to get a feel of the importance of these elements and the reason why companies and individuals need to conduct this basic analysis to support decision-making. Having an understanding of the internal environment will assist entrepreneurs and business managers to arrange resources and internal activities to capitalise on market and external opportunities or threats. It is always interesting to speak to business people who have a vision or set objectives and if you look at the equivalent internal structure or resource allocation you will not be surprise to find they will never achieve these visions or objectives as they have not taken the time to understand their own internal situation. As an entrepreneur, it's crucial to understand your current situation and what needs to be done to move you to your desired state.

Debate

Debate with your employees and team members your current position concerning some of the basic internal elements businesses and entrepreneurs need to consider in response to the external environment:

- Financial resources – do you have access to funding? What other investment opportunities exist and what other sources of income are available to you or your organisation?
- Physical resources – is the location of your business beneficial to your opportunities and objectives? What equipment do you have and what facilities are available?
- Human resources – number of employees, skills level, who is your target market, could you make use of part-time workers or volunteers, do you have a strong influence from the unions?
- Access to natural resources – do you or your organisation hold any patents, copyrights or trademarks?
- Current processes – do you have current internal programs running for employees, software system updates, and departmental hierarchies?

Watch: 📹 **Marketing Briefs TV: Internal Business Analysis – YouTube** Watch this comprehensive 15:42-minute video by Tony Marino, **Marketing Briefs TV: Internal Business Analysis**, *https://www.youtube.com/watch?v=1OEHyDBNrWM*

(28)

Do 👆

As already, indicated entrepreneurs and business managers need to understand the internal factors that have an influence on their businesses and more so have an action plan in place to capitalise on these internal business' influences in response to the external environment. Key to success in this regard is firstly to understand the level of influence and secondly to be able to respond with speed, faster than your competitors. View the following elements level of influence internally on your current or proposed business opportunity and the speed at which you could respond to these factors.

Internal factors that affect business	Level of Impact			Speed at which you could respond	
	Low	Medium	High	Slow	Fast
Customers					
Employees					
Distribution channels and suppliers					
Competitors					
Investors					
Media and general public					

5 - Point plan

Understanding the importance of some of the elements of the micro or internal environment of a business that will assist entrepreneurs in its planning process to develop new business or to stay on course with existing activities. The internal environment is the specific or the task environment of a business, which affects its working or operations directly on a regular basis. Consider the importance of the following factors on your business:

- Customers - no organisation can survive without customers and consumers. A customer is the one who buys a product or service for the consumer who ultimately consumes or uses the product or service of the organisation.
- Organisation culture - an organisation would be a group of all individuals working in different capacities and the collective practices and culture they follow.
- Market – no organisation could exist without a market (system of contact between an organisation and its customers).
- Suppliers – are the providers of inputs like raw materials, equipment and services in to an organisation. Without supplier's organisations are not able to exist.
- Distribution channels – organisations could select to go directly to the market or make use of intermediaries that include agents and brokers who facilitate the contact between buyers and sellers for a commission.

Read

Read and enjoy an article written by Subho Mukher jee, **7 Factors Determining the Internal Environment of a Business,** *http://www.economicsdiscussion.net/business-environment/7-factors-determining-the-internal-environment-of-a-business/10099*

(29)

Let us start the process of looking in more detail to some of the factors influencing the internal environment and what could be done to get a better understanding of these factors that could assist us in our planning process.

3.3 Industry - Things to consider

Entrepreneurs and business managers use industry analysis to determine if they want to enter a product or service market. Careful analysis of several aspects of the industry will determine if you can make a profit selling goods and services in a selected market. Analysing economic factors, supply and demand, competitors, future conditions and government regulations will help you to decide whether to enter an industry or invest elsewhere.

Debate

In discussion with team members it is important for entrepreneurs or business manager to understand the industry in which they operate and its own position in that industry relative to its current or potential competitors. Indicated below are a few simple questions, which should frequently be used in building an understanding of the process:

- Which industry are we in?
- What is the size of the industry?
- Who are the main players in the industry?
- What is our position in the industry, are we a small medium or a leading player?
- What are the benchmarks in the industry and with what do we need to comply?
- How structured are we to enable us to be competitive in the industry?

- Are we in a growing industry or is the industry in a decline phase?

Watch: Industry Analysis – YouTube

Watch this short 6.29-minute video by Corporate Bridge, **Industry Analysis,** *https://www.youtube.com/watch?v=C8rUL4q8evw*

(30)

Do

Everything in your industry that happens outside of your business will affect your current activities or future growth initiatives. The more you know about your industry, the more advantages and protection you will have. What is your level of understanding of the following elements in your industry?

Industry Elements	Level of understanding of the Industry		
	Low	Average	High
Industry participants			
Distribution patterns			
Competitors			
Buying patterns			

12 - Point plan

Entrepreneurs or business managers starting a new business or entering a new market must consider a robust industry analysis, which reviews a wide range of factors. Consider at least the following points below as the starting point of your industry analysis to the background and current status of your industry:

- Define your industry. Are you describing an industry or a segment in that industry? Alternatively, are you defining a single activity of the industry?
- Describe the size of the industry in monetary-value of sales per year. What has been the trend in the size of the industry in recent years?
- What is the growth forecast for the industry?
- Describe the historic profitability of the industry?
- Describe the stage of the product life cycle of the industry product(s) (rapid growth, mature, etc.).
- For processing and manufacturing industries, list the total processing capacity and the amount of processing capacity used. (Show this for the current period and previous years).
- Describe any developments or problems the industry is experiencing.
- Do supply chains or open markets dominate the industry?
- Which parts of the supply chain are commodities and which are differentiated products?
- How do participants create or extract value at different points in the supply chain?
- Describe how distribution channels in the industry, for example direct sales to customers or sales force, retail, and wholesale will function?
- Identify and define the relevant industry segments should you be targeting a niche market.

Read

Read and enjoy an article written by Shanmukha Rao. Padala and Dr. N. V.S. Suryanarayana, **Industry Analysis,**
http://www.articlesbase.com/industrial-articles/industry-analysis-3187078.html

(31)

3.4 Customers - Things to consider

"Ask your customers to be part of the solution, and don't view them as part of the problem"
Alan Weiss, Author "Million Dollar Consulting"

"The best way to hold customers is to constantly figure out how to give them more for less"
Philip Kotler

Customers are what it is all about? Without customers, we don't have a business and no need for a plan. So why is it important to understand our customer and our customer needs? Entrepreneurs and business managers who understand its customers' needs better than its competitors understanding of the same customer needs and are able to attend to these needs have a better chance of survival. Consumers are complex and many factors influence consumer behaviours and decision-making processes. Entrepreneurs who ignore customer needs and fail to understand customer expectation run the risk of missing opportunities. Business managers and entrepreneurs first need to understand its current or potential customers in order to evaluate the potential of an opportunity and then formulate possible offerings to meet customer needs.

It is surprising when talking to entrepreneurs and even some business managers in large corporations to find out how little they know about their customers or potential markets they foresee growth opportunities in. It is not to say if you have a brilliant innovation and or product that customers will buy it from you – perhaps they don't have a need for your product or service? Entrepreneurs and business managers should spend more time on understanding its current or potential customers and less time on following competitors.

This is why you will be able to identify real customer needs and if you could formulate an offer to attend to these needs, you will have a differentiated offer. We have all heard the saying "The Customer is King"; you can decide for yourself if this is true or not, however as said before; no customer no business.

Debate

With your sales team and non-sales team members, consider the answers to the questions below. This will assist with a better understanding of your level of customer insights and quickly focus everybody's attention on the customer. You will notice that I suggest you also include non-sales people in the debate and the reason for this is that sales is not just the function of sales people; it's everybody in the organisation's job. Everybody in the organisation needs to understand the customers' needs that the organisation serves.

- Who are our customers?
- What are their needs?
- What is the size and make-up of our customer base?
- What do we need to have in place to service and maintain our customer base?
- What is the potential growth of our customer base?
- What is the potential untapped value of our customer base?
- What is our customer expectation from us to make sure we address the customer's social and cultural expectations?
- What is the make-up of the customer's profiles in terms of sex, age, income etc.?

- Why do they buy your product or service?
- When do they buy your product or service?
- Where do they buy your product or service?
- Who are your potential customers?
- What do they use your product or service for?
- What factors influence their buying decision?
- What are the customers' expectations with regards to price, product, distribution and promotional activities?

Watch: Understanding Customer Needs – YouTube

Watch this short 2.10-minute video by Infoteam Sales Process Consulting, **Understanding Customer Needs,** *https://www.youtube.com/watch?v=2C-2v99paQM*

(32)

Watch this 44:35-minute video by Galton College, **Customer Analysis,** *https://www.youtube.com/watch?v=v5M4HZRVDJI*

(52)

Do

In order to improve your incites regarding your current customers answer a few of the basic questions below. It might require you to ask some of the questions directly to your customers. Remember you have no better source of information as feedback than from existing customers.

Probing Suggestions	Formulated responses
Why did customers start buying from you?	
How satisfied are your customers with your products and services?	
Why do existing customers continue to buy from you?	
How would your customer describe your business's strengths and weaknesses?	
Do your customers add value to the products and services you offer?	
Are your customers' expectations in line with their actual satisfaction?	
What additional services do your current customers expect from you?	
Would your existing customers refer business to you?	

Customer factors to consider before entering a new market or bringing a new product or service to customers:

Factors for consideration	Response
Who are your customers?	
What is your customers' need?	
How are your customers addressing this need today, however poorly?	
To what extent is your customers affected by not being able to meet this need effectively?	
What is your proposed solution regarding product, service, or both?	
How will your customers benefit, and can you quantify those benefits?	
How will your business make money?	
How big is your total addressable market?	
Who are your competitors, and how do you compare to them?	
How well does the business fit in with your core competencies?	
How can you involve customers in creating a superior solution?	
Can the business generate sustainably high profits?	

6 - Point plan

Customer analysis is a process that needs to be carried out by small, medium as well as large businesses from time to time and should be the first step in the information gathering process before starting any planning processes. The better customer analysis you do, the more you are in touch with your customers and the better you can meet your customer needs. Information about customers could be beneficial to entrepreneurs or any business manager:

- It will assist you in identifying your best customers, to focus on.
- It might help with the identification of additional products and services that could be sold to existing customers.
- It will highlight areas of customer service that needs improvement.
- Better information about your customers will help with better planning and execution of promotional campaigns.
- Better understanding of customers and their needs will assist in the formulation of customer proposals and offerings that will increase market share.
- In order to increase profitability customer needs will have to be satisfied and customer satisfaction will happen only through customer analysis.

Read

Read and enjoy an article written by Ross Beard, **Why Customer Satisfaction is Important (6 Reasons),**
http://blog.clientheartbeat.com/why-customer-satisfaction-is-important/

(33)

Read and enjoy a post written by Jesamine, **Customer Analysis: How to Effectively Target the Market,**
https://blog.udemy.com/customer-analysis/

(53)

3.5 Suppliers - Things to consider

"More and more companies are reaching out to their suppliers and contractors to work jointly on issues of sustainability, environmental responsibility, ethics, and compliance"
Simon Mainwaring

"Companies have to recognize that environmental compliance has become a way of life. Your ability to manage compliance issues has to become part of your supplier management"
Peter West

Suppliers are becoming more and more critical to the execution of any business plan and could influence the success of most growth opportunities. It is critical that entrepreneurs understand the workings of its suppliers, their strengths and weaknesses as well as the willingness of suppliers to partner with businesses to drive growth initiatives. Business managers and entrepreneurs first need to understand their own needs and business plans in order to evaluate suppliers to meet set objectives and criteria that will form part of growth initiatives.

Most suppliers are willing to collaborate with businesses if they understand the plan and expectations. It is also the responsibility of entrepreneurs and business managers to ensure selected suppliers meet expectations. The selection and support of underperforming suppliers will have a detrimental effect on the successful execution of any plan. With the developments associated with the Internet, entrepreneurs are no longer limited to suppliers in local environments only as the internet has opened supplier information to everyone and buyers from individuals to large corporations have access to suppliers who were never available in the past. Also important to keep in mind is that suppliers have choices in terms of whom they select to supply and collaborate with, so entrepreneurs and business managers need to communicate plans and expectations to selected suppliers who are mutually beneficial. Suppliers also keep record of buyer behaviour and might select not to partner with you based on past behaviour.

It is important to understand that a supplier to your organisation or business is a direct extension of your capabilities to deliver products and services to your end customers. Suppliers play a critical role in your success. Entrepreneurs and organisations need to do regular assessments of its suppliers as strong relationships and an understanding of each other's needs and capabilities will assist organisations to plan accordingly. Organisations with a growth agenda need to spend additional time analysing its suppliers for example if you currently operate only in South Africa but plan to develop into the rest of Africa. Would your current suppliers be able to support your operations into Africa? We spoke about building a competitive advantage and being able to charge a premium for that, one of the examples supporting this initiative is Woolworths in South Africa. They stand for quality products meeting specific supplier requirements set by Woolworths, executed by its suppliers.
These requirements form part of Woolworths' supplier analysis criteria. These analyses criteria set by Woolworths are in response to its customer needs.

It is part of its competitive advantage and customers are willing to pay a premium for this differentiation. If customers are not willing to pay a premium for these standards, then do not do it. Whatever your formulated plan and set objectives are it is critical that you regularly review and analyse your suppliers to ensure they meet your criteria and assist in the delivery of your strategic plan and set objectives.

Debate

Understanding current and potential suppliers will be the first priority of entrepreneurs hoping to improve their supply line. A no-growth opportunity dependant on suppliers will not be successful unless the business manager or entrepreneur has done an in-depth evaluation of its suppliers. The evaluation process starts with an evaluation of the current suppliers and a measurement of their capabilities against expectations to support strategies going forward. Discuss with your team members your understanding of the following:

- Who are your suppliers?
- What are their capabilities?
- What are their ethical standards?
- What commercial terms could we arrange with them?
- What infrastructure do they have and what access do they have to technological developments?
- Could we consider backwards integration?
- What guarantees do our suppliers provide for products and services delivered?
- What systems and processes do we have to have in place to make use of the selected suppliers?
- Have we identified alternative suppliers?

Watch: Supplier selection - YouTube

Watch this short 3.15-minute video by SarabandaFashion, **Supplier selection,** *https://www.youtube.com/watch?v=mjWBjw5f0wM*

(34)

Do

The process of supplier evaluation and selection are often complex and will take time. Entrepreneurs and business managers hoping to select the best suppliers to meet growth plans and business objectives need to start with a basic selection and evaluation process. Once done entrepreneurs can move on to more sophisticated processes depending on the complexity of the industry and resources available. Use the table below to get a sense of your current situation and should you have an existing model in place it could also assist in the evaluation and selection of the most suited supplier for your plan.

Things to Consider	Supplier selection Process		
	Yes	No	In Progress
Are you thinking strategically when selecting suppliers?			
Have you identified what you should look for in a supplier?			
Have you been able to identify potential suppliers?			
Have you been able to draw up a shortlist of suppliers?			
Have you started the process of choosing a supplier or suppliers?			
Are you getting the right suppliers for your business strategy?			

5 - Point plan

Having a system or method of supplier evaluation in place will not only assist entrepreneurs to select and collaborate with suppliers that will be able to support selected business strategies and plans but it also holds several other benefits for businesses, such as indicated below. Entrepreneurs or business manager that neglects to select the correct suppliers to support business plans or growth initiatives, run the risk of disappointing customers and stakeholders. Consider some of the benefits below in relation to your current suppliers.

- Reduce business risk and enhance business opportunities.
- Enhance brand recognition and reputation.
- Enhance your ability to strategically plan for the longer term.
- Increase long-term shareholder returns.
- Improve workforce morale and productivity.
- Measure improvements in your productivity activities.
- Save time, improve process and customer relations.
- Benchmark against your competitors and find new customers with a trusted, credible and reliable supplier.

Read

Read and enjoy an article written by Brad Egeland, **Choosing a Vendor: Six Steps to Find the Best Supplier,**
http://www.businessknowhow.com/manage/choosevendor.htm

(35)

3.6 Competitors – Things to consider

"The early bird gets the worm, but the second mouse gets the cheese"
Willie Nelson

> *"World trade means competition from anywhere; advancing technology encourages cross-industry competition. Consequently, strategic planning must consider who our future competitors will be, not only who is here today"*
> **Eric Allison**

Understanding your competitors is not a nice to have when constructing a business or marketing plan it is a must. Competitors are not always people or companies competing with the same products or services as what you bring to the market but could represent other activities, competing for the same disposable income of the market you are targeting. For instance, some years back we had no cell phones and gambling was illegal in South Africa. Consumers had fewer choices to divide their disposable income on such things as movies, dinners and other forms of entertainment. Today consumers have many more choices that influence the portion of their disposable income they are willing to spend on entertainment. Business also has the obvious competitors who operate in the same industry or who target the same customer with similar products and or services.

It's important to first identify competitors to your activity and industry, understand their structures, capabilities, products and services, financial position, strategic intent, are they market leaders or followers, niche marketers or simply followers. Be sure to obtain information on their vision and mission statements, what expansion plans do they have and in what time period? What is the size of the organisation concerning employees; do they have access to research and development? Are they the original equipment manufacturer (OEM) or do they act as re-sellers or distributors? Build an understanding of the competitors pricing and distribution models. If possible, build a view with regards to their cost structures etcetera. A better understanding of your competitors will allow you to develop a competitive advantage in the market and will assist in developing growth and defence strategies.

Gathering competitor information is not that difficult and many sources of information could be used as long as it is legal and ethical. Sales people, newspapers, advertisements, customers, suppliers, journal articles and many more are all good sources of information on competitor activities with regards products and services, prices and many other initiatives. Gauging your own activities against competitors will assist in positioning yourself in the market and allow you to plot your competitors in relation to their position in the market. Are they market leaders, followers, disrupters or niche marketers? Given your understanding of your own objectives and the position of your competitors, you are now in a position to formulate competitor strategies. As discussed, we could position ourselves in the market based on our pre-set objectives. This will influence your competitors as per your selected activities.

As markets and opportunities change and come on to the horizon competitors will respond and adjust their behaviour. Organisations need to be aware of these activities and then decide to respond or not. Remember we are also competitors or potential competitors to others in our market and are being monitored. Care should be taken not to be carried away with every activity of competitors to the extent that we follow or respond to all activities. A good understanding of the market in association with a heightened focus on competitors will guide your judgement.

Debate

When evaluating new opportunities or to gauge your own position in the market to competitors discuss answers to the questions below with your team members and for a balanced view test your results with some trusted customers.
- How many competitors do we have?
- What is the size of these competitors and what capabilities do they have?
- What market share do they have?
- Which products and services do they offer that we could consider?

- Are they the market leaders or followers?
- Are they a threat?
- Which customers are they focusing on?
- Do they have a sales force?
- What are the competitor's growth strategies?
- How do we protect ourselves and our customers against attacks from competitors?
- Do we have adequate competitor information?
- Are we in a position to be competitive?

Watch: Understanding Your Competition – YouTube

Watch this short 7:39-minute video by Nial Strickland, **Understanding Your Competition,**
https://www.youtube.com/watch?v=NEfSyDSaXXk

(36)

Watch this short 5:48-minute video by D2D Millionaire, **Do you know your competition?**
https://www.youtube.com/watch?v=ROkCX_8YRww

(54)

Do

When last have you updated your competitor information, and if you are considering new growth opportunities do, you understand your competitors? There are some perfectly legal ways to get below-the-radar competitive information. Discuss with your team your current position and review some of the options below to gather additional information for decision-making purposes:

Options for gathering additional competitor information			
	Yes	No	Next Step
Pay attention to their advertisements			
Visit competitors regularly			
Ask your business colleagues			
Ask their customers/clients			
Be a customer			
Sign up			
Attend a conference			
Check in with your suppliers			
Hire your competition…			
And watch who they are hiring			
Conduct a survey			
Read the local papers			
Play secret shopper			
Browse public documents			
Google your competitor's website			
Explore LinkedIn			
Troll Twitter and Facebook chatter			
Check what is posted on Slide Share			

5 - Point plan

Gathering information on competitors involves taking stock of the number and nature of competitors that present a direct or indirect threat to your business. Analysing this information can provide aspiring entrepreneurs with a clearer understanding of the marketplace conditions in an industry they are considering breaking into or where they want to evaluate current conditions. Below are additional advantages of competitor information:

- Help with the identification of gaps in the market.
- Assists with product development.
- It is a good catalyst for innovation.
- Is an indication of market trends?
- Will assist entrepreneurs with marketing strategies and activities.

Read

Read and enjoy an article written by Tim Berry, **Know Your Competition,** *https://www.entrepreneur.com/article/78596*

(37)

3.7 Distribution channel – Things to consider

"A product with better distribution will always win over a superior product with poor distribution or customer access. It's not fair. It's not right. But it's reality!"
Stephen Davis Managing Director, CXO Advisory Group

Distribution; without it we are not able to get our products and services to our customers. Entrepreneurs and business managers will soon understand that not focusing on distribution channels to meet customer needs and internal cost expectations could lead to business closure or the exciting of new business opportunities. Selecting a distribution channel does not mean you have to do it all yourself or only make use of one specific model. Once customer needs concerning products and services have been established it is important for entrepreneurs to understand distribution methods and models that is available which could be used to meet customer expectations. These selected distribution methods and models also need to be cost effective and aligned with the business vision and mission. With reference to distribution methods for example: road, air, or sea would be dependent on the industry dynamics.

When we refer to distribution channels then of course a variety of options exists from doing it yourself in-house, outsourcing the function via distributors, agents, partners, franchisees and many other channels to select from. The important thing for entrepreneurs or business managers is to understand customers' needs and expectations, understand what business modes and distribution models exist, what is the current industry practise and what is your objectives for growth and development. Once established we could focus on the cost effectiveness of the selected options and how we could use this to our competitive advantage.

Debate

Selecting the correct distribution channel will not only meet customer needs but also add value to your products and services that could ultimately provide you with a competitive advantage. Update your understanding of your current position in relation to the questions below by discussing it with your team members or potential partners for growth initiatives. Distribution channels could make or break a new venture so take time to understand the options available to your business.

- What are the existing distribution channels?
- Do we distribute our own products or do we work via distributors?
- What does the market expect?
- What are our current distribution capabilities?
- What is the market trends regarding distribution channels and the management of these channels?
- How do we get our products and or service to our customers?
- What are the costs related to our distribution network and could it be done differently?
- What are the legal and commercial requirements we have to meet to be able to trade?
- How many people and across which geographical areas do we distribute?
- What is the international benchmark for distribution channels in our industry?

Watch:  What are distribution channels? YouTube

Watch this short 7:39-minute video by LearnLoads, **What are distribution channels?**
https://www.youtube.com/watch?v=JfBbSLaj0Pc

(38)

Do

In order to gather information and build your confidence before selecting a method or model of distribution consider the variables below as the composition of these element on its own and collectively should influence your decisions. Discussions with team members and customers will enrich your understanding on these elements.

Variables influencing channel selection	Current level of understanding			
	Entry level	Established	Advanced	Action required to improve understanding
Products and services				
Market dynamics				
Use of channel members (middlemen) in the industry				
Organisation size				
Marketing Environment				
Competitors and their activities				
Customer Characteristics				
Channel Compensation cost				

4 - Point plan

The overriding considerations when deciding on a distribution model should be influenced by the elements below:

- Sales volumes, distribution channels should assist with the increase of sales volumes.
- Cost of sales, cost of different distribution channels differs and should be carefully monitored and managed.
- Profits, once you know your expected sales from a potential distribution channel, your cost of sales and your price per unit, you can calculate your profit margin per item as well as gross profits.
- Brand, if you already have strong brand equity in the market you need to consider the effect of your distribution channel on your brand as perceived by the customer.

Read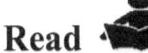
Read and enjoy an article written by Tony Robbins,
DISTRIBUTION CHANNELS,
http://www.referenceforbusiness.com/small/Di-Eq/Distribution-Channels.html

(39)

3.8 Employees – Things to consider

"I have always believed that the way you treat your employees is the way they will treat your customers, and that people flourish when they are praised"
Sir Richard Branson

Employees are the heartbeat of all businesses or at least this is what it is supposed to be. Entrepreneurs and business managers will relate to the fact that they are not able to do everything on their own and that a motivated and caring workforce with the right attitudes and attributes could help build competitive advantages that are difficult to duplicate. Employees are an extension of the business's products and services and are key to manage in accordance to growth opportunities.

Entrepreneurs hoping to grow into a new market or start a new business must be 100% sure of the calibre of people they will need to build the business with, that will add value to customers. Knowing who is needed with what skills and attributes will directly be influenced by the business opportunity, customer needs and business plan objectives. Business managers and entrepreneur who under estimate the value of good competent employees, will soon find out that the market and customers are not tolerant of people who do not meet their needs. Investing in people is an investment into the future.

Debate

Not understanding the business of people and the needs and capabilities of employees would not have an advantage to entrepreneurs or business managers hoping to develop and grow sustainable businesses. Evaluate your basic understanding in debate with team members or human resources practitioners considering your current employees or potential requirements of employees to meet customer needs and business objectives.
- What is the size of our employee complement?
- Do we have the right people to assist us with the execution of our objectives?
- What calibre of people do we need to employ in our system?
- Do our employees belong to unions, if yes which requirements from the unions do we need to abide by?
- Do we need to make use of full time or part time employees?
- What are the benefits we offer our employees?

- What training programs do we have available for our employees?
- Do we attract the best people in the industry?
- Do we have a labour intensive business?

Watch: The Employees First, Customers Second Transformation Journey, YouTube

Watch this short 7:13-minute video by HCL Technologies, **The Employees First, Customers Second Transformation Journey,** *https://www.youtube.com/watch?v=HmV9dmG1XdY*

(40)

Do

Employees are your businesses human capital. With that in mind, we invest in employees and expect a return on investment. In order to evaluate how we go about managing our investment we first need to understand where are we today.

Where are you today?		
	Yes	No
Do you have programs in place to improve leadership development?		
Do you have programs in place to increase employee engagement?		
Do you have programs in place to retain critical talent?		
Do you have programs in place to train and develop employees?		
Do you have programs in place to attract more talent?		
Do you have a human capital management strategy in place?		
Do you have work processes in place?		
Do you have employee feedback mechanisms in place?		
Do you have an understanding of the employee competency requirements?		

5 - Point plan

It is often difficult to identify and find employees that meet the criteria required for the successful implementation and management of business initiatives and to sustain the position over time.

Specific opportunities and entrepreneurial initiatives will require more job specific attributes but in general valuable employees poses the following attributes.
- A positive attitude.
- Good work ethic.
- They are able to take responsibility.
- They are honest with a high level of integrity.
- They are self-motivated, professional and confident.

Read

Read and enjoy an article written by Rita Trehan, **The Importance of Finding the Right Talent,**
https://www.linkedin.com/pulse/importance-finding-right-talent-rita-trehan

(41)

3.9 Media and general public (pressure groups and associations) – Things to consider

"About the press: Never argue with people who buy ink by the gallon"
Tommy Lasorda 1927

Understanding the role of the media and the importance of communities and pressure groups will assist entrepreneurs to influence markets and could have a positive influence on increasing sales and building a positive view of business and potential new ventures.

Some businesses and entrepreneurs believe that their business is too small or the opportunity and activities of a business is not that important to build relationships with the media and communities. This approach could not be further from the truth as these stakeholders could be of enormous value in building perceptions and increasing sales. It is also not true that entrepreneurs or business managers need a big budget to improve relationships with the media. Simple activities managed correctly could generate publicity and influence communities without much effort. Improving relationships and understanding the benefits of leveraging the media in our business activities should be central to our business plan. In today's marketing environment with things like Twitter, Instagram and many other social media platforms entrepreneurs could take control of their own media presence and could influence communities in a controlled manner. A good example of the power of social media is the influence the Twitter platform had in the Trump election campaign in 2016.

Debate

You may have an existing relationship with the media and communities related to your industry or you might be new to this opportunity ensure it is part of your plan by debating some of the questions below with your team. It will provide a snap shot of your current position that might assist in strategic decisions going forward.
- What is our relationship with the media?
- Are they supportive of our activities or do we need to spend time and money for them to portray us in a positive light?
- What form of media do we currently use to communicate with our customers?

- Could we use the media to drive our objectives and to lobby on our behalf?
- Are we aware or are we confronted by pressure groups in our industry or society that we need to manage or use the media to influence?
- What role do the media play in our industry?
- How do we manage and influence the public at large to be positive about our industry and our contribution to society?

Watch: Social Media Marketing - How It Affects Your Business – YouTube

Watch this short 4:25-minute video by, SbrTechnologies Biswajit Singh, **Social Media Marketing -- How it Affects Your Business – YouTube,** *https://www.youtube.com/watch?v=yDA864UskXc*

(42)

Do

Having a good handle on your media presence and being able to influence perceptions and decision-making processes by customers and potential customers is what entrepreneurs strive to achieve with this mechanism (the media) that could be both positive and negative. Consider you and your team's response to the questions below and suggest corrective actions if need be to improve relations with the media or to start building new relationships.

Have you considered the following with regards to your relationship with the media and media selection options			Suggested corrective action
	Yes	No	
What is your business objectives			
What is the cost of the selected media			
Reach or number of people exposed to the message			
Your company's advertising policy and approach			
Type of buyers buying your products			
Conditions under which customers are influenced by the selected media			
Circulation/coverage of the media selected			
Repetition or frequency of the media's exposure			
Credibility and image of the selected media			
Past experience of the selected media			
The selected media's experience of other companies			
Expert Opinion and validation by the selected media			
Type of advertising and other messages you hope to communicate			
How effective is the selected media			
Government rules and regulations applicable to the selected media form			
Availability of the selected media (time and place)			
Type of Products you plan to promote			

5 - Point plan

Social media present great marketing opportunities for entrepreneurs and businesses of all sizes. You can use social media to:
- Promote your brand and business.
- Tell customers about your goods and services.
- Find out what customers think of your business.
- Attract new customers.
- Build stronger relationships with existing customers.
- Differentiate your business from competitors' offerings.

Read

Read and enjoy an article written by Timothy Sykes, **8 Tips to Grow Your Business Using Social Media,**
https://www.entrepreneur.com/article/278598

(43)

3.10 Stakeholders, (investors) relationships – Things to consider

"Relationship-Capital Leaders primary role is to provide their stakeholders CLARITY of Purpose, Plan, and Responsibility"
Rob Peters

Most entrepreneurs understand the value of building relationships with stakeholders both internal and external to business as no business or potential growth opportunity could function without the buy-in and support of stakeholders. Having a plan in place about your vision, mission and objectives will be a powerful tool in the relationship building process with stakeholders. Stakeholders big or small need to be continuously kept up to date with our activities and of course if the community benefit and approve of our behaviour they will support and fight for our existence. Some businesses have excellent relationships with internal and external stakeholders and will testify to the benefit of these support structures in times of crises.

Positive stakeholders will also play a very important function to lobby on your behalf and might even act as a change agent on your behalf. Like all relationships, it needs to be managed and taken care of. Elevate the development and management of these relationships in your strategic process and the benefits will be unmeasurable.

Debate

We all think we have good relationships with so and so, until we test it. To avoid disappointment, review your current relations with stakeholders using the questions below. You will soon have an indication of the current status and entrepreneurs who are serious about their business will work at plans to improve relationships or to capitalise on existing ones.

- Who are all the stakeholders to our industry and company?
- What is our relationship with them?
- What are the trends in building better relationships or how do we maintain our current relationships with our stakeholders?
- Are we a Public, Private or listed company?
- Do we have a listing on the JSE or other stock exchanges?
- What influence do these stakeholders have over market conditions or the company's decision-making process?
- Could we raise more capital via our stakeholders?
- Have we taken all our stakeholders into consideration?

Watch: What is Stakeholder Engagement? - YouTube

Watch this short 3:07-minute video by Future 500, **What is Stakeholder Engagement?**
https://www.youtube.com/watch?v=VHGTsEwbOJY

(44)

Do

In understanding your current relationship status with your stakeholders' entrepreneurs should be able to either take corrective actions to improve relationships or build-on already good relationships as businesses do not operate in isolation.

In order to unlock potential opportunities all stakeholders need to be on-board. Use the table below to evaluate your current status with stakeholders.

Status of current relationship with stakeholders			
Internal			
	Negative	Positive	Action required
Employees			
Management			
Owner/s			
External			
	Negative	Positive	Action required
Suppliers			
Society at large			
Creditors			
Government			
Shareholders			

5 - Point plan

Including stakeholders throughout constant communication and developing positions of mutual respect will assist entrepreneurs and business managers to meet business objectives and grow profits whilst considering the following:

- A company's success depends in large measure on the skill and dedication of its employees,
- Stockholders' initial role is to provide the capital a company needs for growth and expansion.

- The reason for a company's existence is to provide products or services that meet the needs of its target customers and benefit them in a meaningful way,
- A company's ability to fill its customer orders on time and bring the highest quality goods to the marketplace depends in part on the role its vendors or suppliers play,
- The community provides the skilled workforce that a company depends upon to maintain its competitive edge.

Read
Read and enjoy an article written by John Friedman, **Stakeholder Relationships: Key to a Sustainable Enterprise,**
https://www.google.com/url?sa=t&rct=j&q=&esrc=s&source=web &cd=&cad=rja&uact=8&ved=0ahUKEwiwwKjOg93RAhXKD8AK HRfhAlQQFggqMAI&url=http%3A%2F%2Fwww.huffingtonpost. com%2Fjohn-friedman%2Fmanaging-stakeholder-rela_b_1415255.html&usg=AFQjCNGgpPN8cys8zqPJYNp4lZKpI KXH0A

(45)

3.11 Corporate Culture (for existing companies) – Things to consider

"A hallmark of a healthy creative culture is that its people feel free to share ideas, opinions, and criticisms. Lack of candour, if unchecked, ultimately leads to dysfunctional environments."
Ed Catmull, President, Pixar

Corporate culture can take many forms but typically evolve from your business vision and mission statements over time to develop its own unique culture that might consist of things like behaviour, symbols, statements and environment.

Many entrepreneurs strive to create a culture of openness and creativeness in an attempt to differentiate themselves from others and allowing the culture to drive the achievement of set objectives. The culture of an organisation or potential new venture could either assist the growth of an organisation or it could be an obstacle toward further growth and the identification of growth opportunities.

Entrepreneurs and business managers could also be mistaken of the prevailing culture in an organisation that could lead to a miss interpretation of the actual culture and its influence on growth. Whatever shape it takes, your corporate culture plays a big role in determining how well your business will do. It is in your best interest to fully understand your current corporate culture and to change it if needs be in order to meet business objectives and to stimulate creativity.

Debate

Culture in business plays a very important role in the way entrepreneurs will be able to deliver on business objectives and its ability to identify and cultivate new opportunities. For new business ventures, entrepreneurs and business managers might have the opportunity to help shape the potential organisational culture, but for existing businesses it could be a more difficult task.

In line with your business plan, it is important to debate with your team members the response to the questions below as a starting point to support the current culture or to start working on a new culture that will be aligned with your business objectives.

- What is our corporate culture?
- Is it currently a strength or a weakness?
- What value does our culture bring to the business?
- What is our behaviour, because of our corporate culture?
- What are the norms and standards concerning our internal culture?

- Is our culture conducive to growth or do we need to change the current culture?

Watch: What Is Corporate Culture? - YouTube

Watch this short 2:30-minute video by Strategyandbusiness, **What Is Corporate Culture?**
https://www.youtube.com/watch?v=gficoigz1xs

(46)

Do

Use the table below to define your current corporate culture then compare it with your team members' views to clarify your understanding. Afterwards decide to either build onto the existing culture or alternatively set measures in place to change the culture in line with your vision, mission and objectives.

Some corporate cultures		
	Entrepreneurs view	**Employees view**
Team-first corporate culture: Teams first skills and experience second		
Elite corporate culture: Hire the best and want to change the world		
Horizontal corporate culture: Title do not mean much		
Conventional corporate culture: Hierarchies exist		
Progressive corporate culture: Lots of uncertainty		

5 - Point plan

Culture in nations and in business establishes itself from some basic fundamentals and then evolves over time. Entrepreneurs have the ability to influence the fundamentals (setting the tone) derived from business plans that will enable them to influence behaviour. A positive culture could:
- Help the business to attract top talent.
- Help with the creation of passion in the business.
- It supports a competitive advantage.
- It is a form of uniting team members.
- It helps with the retention of talent.

Read

Read and enjoy an article written by Michaek Essany, **6 Ways to Build a Great Corporate Culture for Your Small Business,** *http://quickbooks.intuit.com/r/employees/6-ways-to-build-a-great-corporate-culture-for-your-small-business/*

(47)

3.12 Resource Constrains – Things to consider

"Human resources are like natural resources; they're often buried deep. You have to go looking for them, they're not just lying around on the surface. You have to create the circumstances where they show themselves"
Ken Robinson

Businesses function through the combination of many resources and a lack of the availability of resources or incorrect allocation of resources could severely hamper the continuous success of a business and undermine growth. Many established entrepreneurs will concur by obtaining resources mainly in the form of capital, human or financial and is often the most difficult process in starting new businesses or unlocking growth initiatives.

In most instances, entrepreneurs will find themselves in a position that there is a constraint on available resources and some tuff decisions needs to be made. Understanding which resources are in need for a business opportunity or growth initiative followed by an understanding of the current resources that are available, how they need to be allocated and if needed supported with additional resources.

Entrepreneurs also need to note that some resource requirements might be temporary and others more permanent, which will influence our drive and method of acquisition and distribution.

Debate

Understanding your current resource capability and potential constraints will assist with stakeholder engagements such as the banks or other financial institutions that could assist in overcoming these constraints. Debate with your team members your current position and what needs to be done to meet your business objectives by considering the answers to the questions below.

- What are our current resources?
- Are we constrained or do we have the resources to grow?
- Do we understand what is required from a resources perspective if we plan to expand?
- Who controls the resources and what is the cost associated to our resources?
- What effect does a constraint on resources have on our business?
- In order to grow what resources, do we need?

Watch: 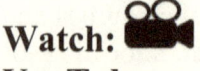 Launching a start-up - Key Resources - YouTube

Watch this short 4:45-minute video by Aamar Aslam, **Launching a start-up - Key Resources**,
https://www.youtube.com/watch?v=oNo2SCHmrIE

(48)

Do

Assessing your resource requirements against your business plan should be done in association with team members. Often there is disconnect between actual requirements in the business and the business manager or entrepreneur's assessment of resource requirements or allocations. First, classify your resource requirement and then indicate the urgency to increase or correctly allocate the identified resource in order to enable your business plan execution.

Resource identification		Level of urgency		
	Yes	Low	Medium	High
Physical assets (buildings, machines, vehicles etc.				
Intellectual know how, patents, brands, partnerships etcetera.				
Human, general human resources / speciality (qualified resources)				
Financial, cash, guarantees, extended credit etcetera.				

5 - Point plan

Once we understand the current position on the availability of resources entrepreneurs needs to make decisions on acquiring additional resources. Consider the following:

- Reliability - downtime caused by unreliability can be detrimental to the success of a small business.
- Cost - remember that the cheapest option may not always be the best for your business.
- Quality - influences factors such as operational efficiency and productivity.
- Value for money - are you getting what you pay for or is there a better alternative available?
- Ongoing support - if your resources require maintenance or other support, do you know how to access it if you need to?

Read

Read and enjoy a post written by David Ehrenberg, **What is the best way to identify the financial, human and physical resource requirements for a business?** *https://www.quora.com/What-is-the-best-way-to-identify-the-financial-human-and-ph*.

(49)

Again, it is clear from the above list that many internal elements need to be reviewed and considered in the analysis of the internal environment. The list of variables has some standard elements that need revision but will differ from company to company. Once the elements of the Micro environment have been listed, examined and reviewed it is time to understand the market analysis and its influence on decision making.

3.13 Market analysis

"The aim of marketing is to know and understand the consumer so well, the product or service fits them and sells itself"
Peter F. Drucker

Understanding the market assist with decision-making. It is critical for entrepreneurs to understand the market and industry they are focusing on. Without analysing the market, it will be impossible to identify potential risk and it would be imposable to build defences to mitigate against potential risk. Market analysis include understanding the size of the market, current trends, new opportunities, what portion of the market you hold and what portion could be seen as an opportunity.

Market analysis is a continuous process of information gathering, analysing, interpreting and processing in an effort to influence decision-making. Most entrepreneurs do market analysis in an informal way and sometimes come to incorrect conclusions. The processes of gathering information and analysing it for decision-making could enable businesses to gain a competitive advantage above competitors.

Debate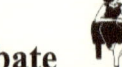

Entrepreneurs or business managers could improve their market analysis capabilities by asking the questions below and start by building up a database of the relevant information. By discussing the responses to the question below with team-members and related role player's entrepreneurs will develop a more holistic formulised view of the market. Remember if your competitors have a more informed and in-depth understanding of the market and its potential it will be difficult for you to compete.

- What are the current trends in the selected market, for example the black middle class in South Africa are currently growing with demand on housing and education?

- What is the size of the market, would it be large enough for additional growth?
- How many players are in the market, how would that influence your marketing activities?
- What is the growth rate in the selected market?
- Is the market saturated or is there still room for new entrants?
- How is the market affected by changing economic or legislation changes?
- What is the disposable income of the average consumers in the market; would they be able to afford your products and services?
- Is the market only identified as local or does it also resonate abroad?
- Who are the major players in the market?
- What are the projected growth patterns for the selected markets?
- What are the barriers to entry into the selected market; are you part of the barriers or are their barriers you need to contend with?

Watch:  **Market analysis - YouTube**

Watch this short 20:00-minute video by Henning Glaser, **Market analysis,** *https://www.youtube.com/watch?v=g5rVxlLPAF8*

(50)

Do

Understanding the markets, you currently operate in or building an understanding of markets to enter would be powerful as it drives decision-making and will assist shareholder orientation and resource allocations. Entrepreneurs should constantly review the variables as per the table below and take corrective actions in areas where a lack of information and understanding exist.

Variables to consider	Action to be taken		
	Yes	No	Next Step
Do we understand the current market size (current and future)			
Do we understand the profitability of the market			
Do we understand the growth rate of the selected market			
Do we understand the cost structure of the market			
Do we understand the current and future distribution structures of the market			
Do we understand the market trends			
Do we understand the key success factors for the selected market			

5 - Point plan

A proper market analysis reveals to entrepreneurs what it must change to meet the market's needs more profitably. It identifies how the business can reach its potential consumers and appeal to their needs. Conducting a market analysis also helps businesses identify when to discontinue products, it also helps with the following:

- Market analysis will assist businesses with target market selection.
- It assists with decisions on product positioning and strategy setting.
- It will guide product positioning and strategy formulation.
- It could help a business to avoid potential losses.

- It influences decision-making.

Read

Read and enjoy a post written by Joy Levin, **How Marketing Research Can Benefit a Small Business,**
https://smallbiztrends.com/2006/01/how-marketing-research-can-benefit-a-small-business.html

(51)

3.14 Swot analysis

"A SWOT analysis involves asking, what are our strengths and weaknesses? What are our opportunities? What are the threats?"
Amanda Lang

Entrepreneurs and business managers in general will agree, without a solid understanding of your own strengths, weaknesses opportunities and threats it is pointless to even start thinking of constructing or executing a business plan.

Lots have been said about the so-called swot analysis but in essence it resolves about an in-depth understanding of yourself as an individual or an organisation by yourself. When constructing your swot analysis, you need to be open and honest about your capabilities and limitations. It is also important to be balanced in your assessment of threats and opportunities.

Not all threats are real threats to yourself or your organisation and not all opportunities are real opportunities given your own capabilities and resource constrains. For example: If you are in the fast food industry in South Africa and you run a small fast food outlet then franchising your business sounds like a good opportunity but ask yourself – at this moment in time do I have the resources and knowhow to make good on this opportunity or is this more of a longer term opportunity.

It is important for entrepreneurs to dream big and drive individual aspirations, doing so will be even better served with a solid understanding of a business's swot analysis. What is the value of a swot analysis for a business or individual?

Debate

Debate your organisation's competitive advantages derived from the completion of your organisations swot analysis. The worst thing entrepreneurs and organisations can do is to complete a swot analysis and do nothing with the information constructed. You need to take action and make decisions.

- What are you going to do about your strengths identified?
- What are the next steps in improving on some of your weaknesses listed?
- Would you be able to do anything about the identified threats?
- How do you plan to capitalise on your strengths and build them in to competitive advantages?
- How do you plan to develop your opportunities and by when?

8 - Point plan

Most entrepreneurs and business managers have a good understanding at least in their own minds concerning their businesses strengths, weaknesses, threats and opportunities. However, it is only when these assumptions are being tested and further developed (by the inputs of customers and others) that the real value of a swot analysis will emerge. Below are some of the additional benefits a well develop swot analysis will contribute to:

- It focusses activities during the analysis process to getting all stakeholders involved.
- It assists with strategic planning, as all strategic departments are required to participate in the analysis process, sales, marketing, management, workers and executives.
- It is an honest reflection of an organisation's capabilities, and constrains.
- It will assist management to make decisions.
- It will assist management with risk management.
- It will assist the organisation and individual entrepreneurs to focus on growth areas and resource it accordingly.
- It will be clear on current and potential threats; this might be in the form of an aggressive competitor or advances in technology.

Watch: Putting Your SWOT to Work - YouTube

Watch this short 3:46-minute video by Elsa Ozuna Richards,
Putting Your SWOT to Work,
https://www.youtube.com/watch?v=exm9uAKYkl0

(55)

Do

Make a list of your own Strengths, Weaknesses, Opportunities and Threats using the table below: Once done ask a friend, family member and a colleague to add or delete from your analysis. After completion decide on the next steps – what will you be focusing on to improve, develop and avoid?

Strengths:	Opportunities:
Weaknesses:	Threats:

In order to differentiate a business and its offerings it needs to build a competitive advantage amongst its competitors in the market. Competitive advantages are those things that come in the form of perhaps products and services, infrastructure, technical expertise and so forth, which makes you or your organisation different.

Differentiation is often the reason why customer buy from you – use the swot analysis process to identify your competitive advantage. Once done the challenge is to then understand it and to drive an agenda that will assist you to capitalise on the advantage. You should be able to obtain a premium for your competitive advantage, if not; it is not a competitive advantage.

Read

Read and enjoy an article written by Julia Padget, **What is SWOT analysis and how can it add value?**
https://www.linkedin.com/pulse/what-swot-analysis-how-can-add-value-julia

(56)

The completion of a personal or business swot analysis will also assist entrepreneurs and organisations with the process of prioritisation to decide what is critical and needs urgent attention.

This could be difficult as businesses are often complex with many variables and activities preventing the organisation to focus on its core activities and exploiting its real opportunities.

"Our strength grows out of our weaknesses"
Ralph Waldo

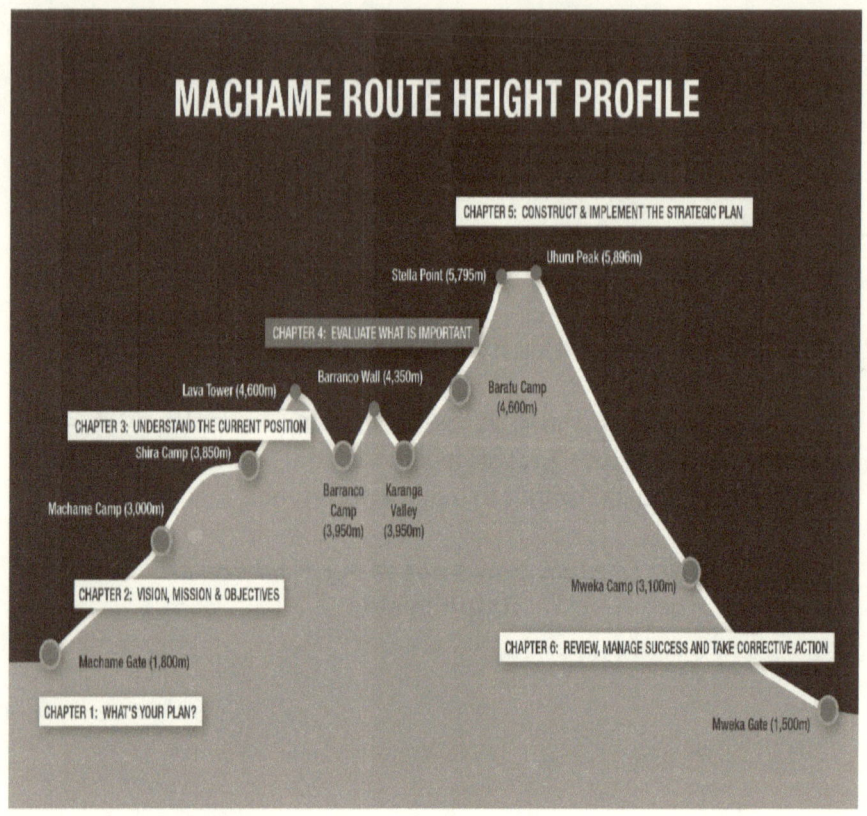

Personal Journey: Barranco Camp – Barafu Camp
Day 4 on mountain
Barranco Camp – Barafu Camp 3,985m (13,071ft) – 4,681m (15,358ft)
Average hiking time: 7 hours
From Barranco Camp you will start ascending the Barranco Wall (100m – very steep) and continue hiking to Karranga Valley. Enjoy your packed lunch and refill your water bottles, as this is your last water point. The vast and barren moonscape of the alpine desert is a very harsh and rugged environment. Only tussock grasses and a few tiny flowers can survive at this altitude. Uhuru Peak sometime hauls itself through the clouds and it seems very close. **Overnight at Barafu Camp**

Chapter 4: Evaluate what is critical

"When you write a book, you spend day after day scanning and identifying the trees. When you're done, you have to step back and look at the forest"
Stephen King, On Writing: A Memoir of the Craft

When formulating a strategic business or marketing plan we need to evaluate all the relevant variables and make decisions on what is critical and what is less important. Making decisions is the ability to think clearly and rationally about what to do or not to do. It includes the ability to engage in reflective and independent thinking. Up until this stage of the plan-formulating process entrepreneurs and organisations were in the information gathering phase and it is now time to evaluate what are critical items to focus on and make decisions of selection. This follows onto the next steps to develop opportunities and to mitigate risk.

Debate

Entrepreneurs need to debate with team members the success of its strategic plans by evaluating the impact and performance of each element. Below find a list for discussion and evaluation. Remember to only evaluate and action critical elements to your plans' success. If your plan is not working you might have to do some more analysis and re-formulate your plan to focus on the critical elements:

Critical elements of your plan for evaluation	Yes	No	Corrective action
Do you understand the key factors that affected the business for good or for bad during the past year?			
Do you keep customer satisfaction scores and the number and type of customer complaints?			
Do you have information on the satisfaction levels of distributors, retailers, and other value chain members?			
Marketing programs are marketed internally and "bought into" by top managers and non-marketing teams?			
The offering: Has the customer' needs been met as expected, and were the offerings competitor advantage defensible?			
Did the performance of the organisation's advertising, promotion, sales, marketing, and research programs support the return on the money invested in them?			
Did the individual elements of the marketing plan achieve their stated financial and nonfinancial goals?			

Watch: Strategic Plan Review – Cowlitz County - YouTube

Watch this short 8:49-minute video by Kevin Hunter, **Strategic Plan Review – Cowlitz County,** *https://www.youtube.com/watch?v=SGtLEWTzimc*

(57)

Do

Evaluating what is critical remains the responsibility of the entrepreneur or business manager who is the owners of the strategic plan. The evaluation could take the form of many elements but all needs to be relevant to the objectives of the plan: a contribution to the success of the plan. Below are some suggestions of common elements of strategic plans evaluated over time. Discuss your plan while evaluating in response to these factors.

- What was the return on investment?
- Did the plan deliver on the sales or revenue numbers?
- What response did you get from customers?
- Did you experience an increase in expansion activities or growth?
- What response did you get from you partners or stakeholders?
- What response did you get from your salespeople?
- What response did you get from competitors?

5 - Point plan

In order to make critical decisions entrepreneurs need to have specific decision making skills. Someone with critical decision-making skills is able to:

- Understand the logical connections between ideas.

- Identify, construct and evaluate arguments.
- Detect inconsistencies and common mistakes in reasoning.
- Solve problems systematically including identifying the relevance and importance of ideas.
- Reflect on the justification of one's own beliefs and values.

Making decisions come with consequences and mitigating against decisions posing a high risk should form part of an entrepreneur's decision-making process. Having a strategic plan in place is one of the fundamental processes of mitigating risk and improving rewards.

Read

Read and enjoy an article written by Rich Horwath, **5 Critical Moments to Evaluate Your Strategy,**
http://www.skipprichard.com/5-critical-moments-to-evaluate-your-strategy/

(58)

4.1 Target market selection

"Understand why you are different and how you help, recognise your target market, and give them something they might not even realise they are missing"
Author: Chris Murray

Before selecting a target market, entrepreneurs and organisation's first need to understand the profile of selected target markets. What is the profile of the target market? For example, are they male or female, middle income or high income? What is the age group of the target market? How does the target market make buying decisions? What is the spending pattern of the target market?

How do you need to communicate with the target market? What are the growth patterns of the target market and so forth? Business will evaluate different segments based on its expectations concerning growth patterns, margin expectations and geographical location.

Once the different profiles of the selected target markets are drawn-up entrepreneurs will have to make decisions on which target market or markets they will focus on going forward. It is seldom recommended to focus on all target markets identified due to the constraint of available resources. The organisation should also only select target markets that are in line with their objectives and growth agenda. For organisation's to capitalise on the benefits of selected target markets they need to understand the needs of its selected target market and develop products and services that will attend to its selected market's needs.

Debate

Review the profile of your current selected target market/s in discussion with your team members and stakeholders to evaluate if they meet your strategic plan objectives and if they are critical to the execution of your strategic plan.

	Yes	No	Next Steps
Are you able to state your target market and the needs you will be fulfilling?			
Which new and potential target markets have you identified that is critical to focus on?			
What additional resources would be required to service these selected target markets?			
What is the expected return on investment out of these target markets?			
Have you been able to break this large market down into smaller sections (segmentation)?			
Have you developed your customer profile?			
Now that you have fully identified your target market, have you done research to verify that there will be enough business in this group to support your company in its growth process?			
Have you done research to determine the market size and potential market share?			

Selecting the correct target market will have a fundamental influence on the success of any organisation and getting it wrong is not an option. Entrepreneurs should take great care during the evaluation and selection process. Remember target market identification and selection is not the sole domain of one organisation, it is more likely that others have selected the same target markets making it even more difficult to have a competitive advantage as perceived by selected target markets.

Watch: How to Identify Target Market | Target Market Examples -YouTube

Watch this short 7:00-minute video by Network Marketing Success, **How to Identify Target Market | Target Market Examples,** *https://www.youtube.com/watch?v=hE5z7essD7E*

(59)

Do

We have already established the importance of being able to select a target market to focus on and the benefits that entrepreneurial businesses could gain from focusing on selected target markets. As a general check review the answers to the questions below and if most of them are negative, suggest some corrective actions or next steps to drive the target market selection-process.

Quick questions on the status of your target market selection			
	Yes	No	Next Steps
Have you picked a specific type of product or service to focus on?			
Have you narrowed down your niche? Using the previous examples above, specify niches			
Have you been able to solve your target market's problem with your products or services?			
Ask yourself whether your target market can afford to buy what you are selling?			
Research the type of media your target market frequently pays attention to			
Have you analysed your competitors?			

5 - Point plan

As an entrepreneur, choosing a specific target market for your business is a powerful form of focus. Targeting means you reject the idea of believing the best way to build your business is by engaging with every living person in your area. It allows you to focus on the specific customer or client types that are most desirable. Below are some of the most common benefits of focusing on a specific target market:

- You will eliminate the bottom-feeders and those people who will simply not value what you offer.
- You will have more effective marketing spend.
- You can better focus your messaging-tailored to focus on their needs, not the needs of the entire universe.
- It is a better use of your time-more spent serving your best customers and less time spent pursuing low-value prospects.
- You will build a stronger referral base-once you penetrate a target market and educate them on the value of working with you.

Read

Read and enjoy an article written by April Dunford, **Start-up Market Segmentation: 5 Steps to Selecting a Target Market,** *http://www.rocketwatcher.com/blog/2015/04/startup-market-segmentation.html*

(60)

4.2 Market strategies – building a competitive advantage

"An organization's ability to learn, and translate that learning into action rapidly, is the ultimate competitive advantage"
Jack Welch

Most entrepreneurs and organisations will agree that to differentiate yourself from competitors is one of the most difficult things to do in business. However, one of the methods to use could be to identify some elements, products or services that differentiate your offer to the market from that of others.

Many factors could be evaluated such as, your technical capabilities, range of products offered, quality of products offered, extent of after sales service and geographical locations. These elements could assist in your attempt to differentiate yourself from your competitors. Building a competitive advantage is making use of these elements of differentiation to establish yourself as having a competitive advantage in the minds of customers.

Only customer's perceptions of your offering will qualify whether you hold a competitive advantage or not. It is not worth having a competitive advantage if customers are not willing to pay a premium for it. Many elements within a marketing or sales campaign could be used to build a competitive advantage however, these activities will cost money and if it's not supportive of your overall plan and strategy and you don't get a proper return on your investment then do not spend time exploring them.

Debate

Debate with your team members: What is your competitive advantage; review some contributing elements. Is it still relevant? What do your customers perceive your competitive advantage to be? Is it worth your while to develop additional focus via marketing programs to highlight your competitive advantages and are you able to demand a premium for your competitive advantages?

Do you know what your competitive advantage will be before you start your new venture and most importantly will you be able to influence the potential consumers to pay for all the "bells and whistles"?

Watch:  How to Develop Competitive Advantage - YouTube

Watch this short 3:31-minute video by Erica Olsen, **How to Develop Competitive Advantage**, *https://www.youtube.com/watch?v=S9O2oPbT3fs*

(61)

Do

Developing a sustainable competitive advantage takes time and effort from everyone involved. Find time to discuss the issues below with your teams and start driving internal behaviour to becoming more differentiated in support of gaining a competitive advantage.

- Understand the market and its segments. Look for those niches that are not well serviced by competitors and can be profitably targeted and sold to.
- Develop an understanding of what customers really want and establish a value proposition that grabs their attention.
- Work out the key things that you need to do really well to support and deliver the value proposition, e.g. service levels, quality, branding, pricing, etcetera.
- Understand what your strengths and core competencies are and how you can use these in innovative ways to provide value to your chosen market.
- Design your business model to support and deliver the value proposition.

5 - Point plan

The importance of having a competitive advantage could be well described by the comments below.
Entrepreneurs and business managers focusing on building a competitive advantage that delivers superior value to their customers ahead of competitors will increase sales and profits over a longer and more sustainable period.

- It is the heart of marketing strategy.
- It is the antidote for competitor's superiority.
- It is the route to the long-term marketing success.
- It makes profit a secondary product.
- It makes the business unit to remain competitive evergreen.

Read

Read and enjoy an article written by Peter Voogd, **5 Ways Entrepreneurs Can Gain a Competitive Advantage,**
https://www.entrepreneur.com/article/243717

(62)

4.3 Product strategies – review product and company life cycle status

"Don't find customers for your products, find products for your customers"
Seth Godin

As all good things in life, we all have a time to come and a time to go. Products and organisations are also exposed to a cycle of activities with certain characteristics being reflective of the phase in which the products or organisations finds themselves.

For a product they refer to the introduction phase where the product is not that well known and entrepreneurs and organisations need to spend time and money to get the product to be noticed and to establish it in new markets. Once introduced, the product will move into the growth phase during which the demand for the product will increase and the organisations resources are tested.

Organisations and entrepreneurs need to adjust expectations during this phase as bigger demands exist regarding the capabilities of organisations to be able to deliver during this growth phase. For some organisations moving through these different phases happens quickly and for others it might take longer depending on the target markets selected and marketing programs supporting the strategic plans.

The stable phase of the product life cycle normally indicates that the product is well known to its current and potential customers with positive sales being generated over a prolonged period. This phase also allows organisations to recover some of the capital spent during the first two phases. Organisations and entrepreneurs need to make the best of this phase to prolong or avoid the decline phase. Products that move into the decline phase tend to lose their market position against competitors and form part of the group of products that needs protection against the decline in sales and competitor attacks.

Organisations and entrepreneurs should take corrective action to avoid products from moving from the stable phase to the decline phase. The same principle applies to start-ups and established businesses. Life cycle is a fact of business and needs to be foreseen in order to manage the risks. Entrepreneurs and organisations need to understand its product and company status with regard to the different phases of the life cycles in order to be more effective marketers and to influence the potential outcomes.

It is also important to understand competitor positions with respect to their products or organisational status as depicted in the life cycle theory. Having a holistic overview of these cycles will assist entrepreneurs and organisations to formulate its own behaviours and actions relative to the phase they find themselves in or the aspirational position they aspire to. Moving between phases within these cycles often requires a behavioural change and as indicated earlier, changing behaviour is one of the most difficult tasks of business. Without a plan and strategy, this will not be possible.

Debate

Debate the status of your current product or service offer into the market with your team members, stakeholders and customer. The same process could be used to evaluate the current status of your business or for the evaluation of competitive products in the market. Understanding what phase of the life cycle you find yourself in will influence decision making and the next steps. The exercise could be done per individual product or product grouping.

Product Life Cycle Phase	Selected Product		
	Yes	No	Next Steps
Market introduction			
Growth			
Maturity			
Decline			

Watch: The Product Life Cycle - YouTube

Watch this short 6:34-minute video by Alanis Business Academy, **The Product Life Cycle,**
https://www.youtube.com/watch?v=KVMTMfCO1dY

(63)

Do

Entrepreneurs understanding the phase of the product life cycle can find their products in need to decide whether to stay in the current phase for as long as possible given competitive activities or economic pressures or to take steps to move to the next phase. Review with your teams the characteristics associated with the phases identified in the previous exercise and decide on the next steps. Not understanding your position in the life cycle could be costly and leave you vulnerable to the competition.

Product Life Cycle Phase	Selected Product			
	Yes	No	Characteristic of phase	Understand what needs to be done to maintain position or to move to the next phase
Market introduction			Little or no competition	
Growth			Cost begin to decline as economics of scale kick in	
Maturity			Sales volumes reaches a peak; further competition enter the market	
Decline			Sales volumes decline, prices fall further	

5 - Point plan

Entrepreneurs and business managers that understand their products, organisation and competitors' products current life-cycle positions will benefit as this will influence decision making around costs and market growth. Below find some of the benefits businesses can enjoy with strategic and well thought out Product Life Cycle Management:

- It reduces time to the market.
- Its reduce market entry costs.
- It assists with the development of more efficient and profitable distribution channels.
- It helps with the generation of higher returns from investments from promotional campaigns.
- It extends the lifetime of your product by adapting your approach as it moves through the lifecycle and will assist with the orderly and profitable end of life product management.

Read

Read and enjoy an article written by Note Desk, **Product Life Cycle (PLC),** *http://www.notesdesk.com/notes/marketing/product-life-cycle-plc/*

(64)

4.4 Relationship strategies – review relationship maps

"You can make more friends in two months by becoming interested in other people than you can in two years by trying to get other people interested in you"
Dale Carnegie

Entrepreneurs and business managers understand that no business or business opportunity functions on its own. We all need to be able to identify our stakeholders and start building relationships that will support us in the tuff times. After the identification of our stakeholders, we need to formalise a formal document declaring the relationship we hope to build with an individual, organisation, internal and external customers.

Having specific objectives of what we want out of the relationship will drive our behaviour and those of others. Entrepreneurs hoping to move customers from transactional activities to partnership relations need to identify the relationships they need to build and develop in order to reach the set objective. Relationship maps capture the associated information and allocate a responsible person from your business or environment tasked to build specific relationships. Entrepreneurs hoping to be successful engage in relationship-building activities in order to gain something from the relationship. Building and development of relationships could be with more than one stakeholder or customer simultaneously and with the sole purpose of gaining new business.

Entrepreneurs need to define the process of capturing information about stakeholders and devise a strategy to set relationship objectives, and then drive the plan. Business relationships should be supportive of set objectives and result in a win-win result for the business and stakeholders. Sometimes without the identification of all the stakeholders and the building of relationships, organisations might be unaware of areas where important relationships need to be build.

Debate

Entrepreneurs and business managers together with their teams often hold relationships with many stakeholders and might not leverage these relationships optimal in line with their business objectives and initiatives.

It is therefore important that businesses have a central platform for the registration of relationships and delegate responsibilities for the development of these relationships to the most appropriate person in the business that will drive specific relationship objectives. Making use of a relationship map with defined ownership and objectives will assist in the achievement of relationship objectives. Some suggested activities below might assist in the development and improvement of existing and potential business relationships to consider your current position:

Suggestions to improve on business relationships	Yes	No	Corrective Actions
Do you encourage honest feedback?			
Do you listen more than you talk?			
Do you make it part of your routine?			
Do you focus on being honest?			
Do you take notes?			
Do you give more than you receive?			
Are you being proactive?			
Are you always real?			
Do you turn blunders into opportunities?			
Do you make it personal?			
Do you meet face to face?			

Watch:  **Introduction to stakeholder maps - YouTube**

Watch this short 4:55-minute video by LearnLoads, **Introduction to stakeholder maps,**
  https://www.youtube.com/watch?v=bOIT1GKVMd8

(65)

Do

During the relationship-building process, entrepreneurs and business managers endeavour to move a customer up the loyalty ladder from transactional relationships to partnership relations.

Having a partnership relationship with customers and stakeholders will call for engagement and commitment from both parties. Find some suggestions below that entrepreneurs and their teams could implement to assist with relationship building objectives:

- Entrepreneurs and sales teams need to connect with influencers.
- Find the right stakeholder networking groups.
- Offer something of value to your stakeholders.
- Take accountability for your relationships and hold team members responsible for predefined deliverables.
- Create your own opportunities and take your stakeholders along.

5 - Point plan

It is important that entrepreneurs understand the value of building relationships but at the same time also follow some guidance in the process of building relationships with key stakeholders in order to influence and drive change. See some suggestions below:

- Aim to build strong relationships early on with the key decision makers.
- Seek advice and assistance from more positive stakeholders.
- Regularly meet with key stakeholders who are resistant to change, involve and consult with them so that their concerns are voiced and at the same time take the opportunity to re-emphasise the benefits of change.
- Agree how and when you will communicate.
- Share your early project plans and keep surprises to a minimum!

Read

Read and enjoy an article written by Deborah Shane, **11 Ways to Build Solid, Strong, Lasting Business Relationships,**
https://smallbiztrends.com/2015/06/build-lasting-business-relationships.html

(66)

4.5 Competitive strategies

"A company's ability to respond to an unplanned event, good or bad is a prime indicator of its ability to compete"
Bill Gates

Having a competitive strategy in place will assist entrepreneurs and business managers to manage competitors, always have a backup plan in place. Competition is good and one of the principals of a free market system however it could be costly to maintain. Entrepreneurs and business managers are thus encouraged to formulate their own competitive strategy based on several factors from differentiation and low cost operations to a focused approach.

The selections are not made in isolation as we always need to be aware of our competitor's activities but our selections should be based on our understanding of the market and customer needs in line with our selected strategic marketing plan. Competitive strategies describe what it is that we would be focusing on and how we will formulate our USP (unique selling proposition). Being competitive based on customer needs typically leads to an increase in sales and profitability.

Debate

Entrepreneurs and business managers planning to be competitive need to debate the status of their current competitive strategies and might have to consider a change in direction for the penetration of new markets or opportunities. Below are some common competitive strategies for review and consideration, (remember whatever the current status; it needs to be evaluated against changes in the market and strategic market plan objectives).

Current competitive strategy	Yes	No	Corrective Action (in line with strategic marketing plan)
A low-cost leader strategy: striving to be the overall low-cost provider of a product or service that appeals to a broad range of customers			
A broad differentiation strategy: seeking to differentiate the company's product offerings from rivals in ways that will appeal to a broad range of buyers			
A best-cost provider strategy: giving customers more value for their money by emphasising both low cost and upscale differences, the goal being to keep costs and prices lower than those of other providers of comparable quality and features			
A focused, or market-niche, strategy based on lower cost: concentrating on a narrow buyer segment and outcompeting rivals on the basis of lower cost			
A focused, or market-niche, strategy based on differentiation: offering niche members a product or service customised to their tastes and requirements			

Watch: Competitive Strategy in 3 Minutes - YouTube

Watch this short 3:29-minute video by Prof Joe Urbany, **Competitive Strategy in 3 Minutes,**
https://www.youtube.com/watch?v=bl5cyZlay4k

(67)

Do

Entrepreneurs and business managers often find themselves isolated in thinking and evaluating business options. Expand this process when thinking and developing competitive strategies. Consider the elements below in discussion with your teams and customers in order to better existing competitive strategies and to develop new creative strategies.

Elements of successful competitive strategies	Yes	No	Next steps
Do you know the competition?			
Do you know your customers?			
Are you differentiating your products and services?			
Have you already stepped up your marketing activities?			
Is it time to update your image?			
Do you look after your existing customers?			
Are you targeting or planning to target new markets?			
Are you expanding your offer?			
Are you the best employer?			
Do you look to the future?			

5 - Point plan

Competitive strategies for entrepreneurs and business managers should be a talking point and part of their daily activities. Without a competitive strategy, businesses and start-ups will merely follow competitors, not being able to differentiate and build a long-term sustainable business. Competitive strategies should be developed on some of the fundamental foundations as shared below:

- If you have real intellectual property, you need to protect it.
- Build your strategy on a dynamic product line, rather than a single product.
- Make sure you show dramatic cost improvements.
- Build your teams with inside relationships and experience.
- Lock onto the market or customer base with a strong focus and differentiation.

Read

Read and enjoy an article written by Ed Hatton, **Competitive Strategy,** *http://www.entrepreneurmag.co.za/advice/business-leadership/strategy/competitive-strategy/*

(68)

4.6 Brand strategies – building value

"A great brand is a promise, a compact with a customer about quality, reliability, innovation, and even community. And while the concept of brand is intangible, brand equity is far from it"
Stephen B. Shepard

Entrepreneurs and business managers alike should not underestimate the value of a brand, with a brand being more than just a logo or slogan. Brand strategies involve the identification of core values that the selected brand needs to represent, in association with the logo, slogans, colours and brand positioning activities that will support a business's brand strategy. Entrepreneurs should evaluate their current brand strategies to understand if it is supportive of its strategic marketing plans or representative of new initiatives in markets to be developed or opportunities to be unlocked.

Brands and brand strategies need to be a reflection of the values of the entrepreneur or its business and must support positioning strategies. Brand positioning strategies refer to how entrepreneurs and businesses would like to position themselves in the market relative to its competitors in the minds of customers. Brand and ultimately brand strategies are a very powerful tool that entrepreneurs could control to influence perceptions and consumers buying behaviours. What is your brand strategy?

Debate

When you have the company's core brand values well-defined, and you've worked through your messaging and you have engaged your whole organisation in producing them, it produces a really strong, cohesive vision. Everybody is singing from the same song sheet. Entrepreneurs need to constantly evaluate and ensure its brands strategies are supportive of its selected core values.

What are your core values?

Debate with your teams if your current brand strategy is representative of your core values?

Next steps and or corrective action. Maintain or change course
----

Watch: What is "BRAND STRATEGY"? – YouTube

Watch this short 3:29-minute video by Gavin Wedell, **What is "BRAND STRATEGY"?** *https://www.youtube.com/watch?v=H-RaxV2as8s*

(69)

Do

Brand strategy variables are elements of a brand strategy that the entrepreneur or business manager have direct control over – remember it is your values, your brand and your brand strategy so you should ensure that you control the brand positioning at all times to meet set brand objectives. Consider the variables below and plan your brand strategy and position to gain the most out of your selected brand.

Brand strategy variables	Yes	No	Next steps and or Corrective actions
Does your brand and brand strategy resonate with your target audience?			
What is your brand promise and does your target audience understand the promise?			
Is there a positive perception about your brand in the market?			
Have you clarified and communicated your brand values to your target audience?			
Does your brand have a personality?			
Is your brand positioning in line with your brand objectives?			

5 - Point plan

Brand strategies do not develop themselves and need some input from entrepreneurs, business managers, team members and perhaps some customers. It is a creative process and without help in this regard or a lack of creativity consider the guidance below during the brand strategy development process.

- Successful business brands are built on a long-term strategy, not a short-term campaign.
- Perhaps sell an experience and not just a name.
- Collaborative internal branding leads to a successful brand creation process.
- Businesses need to tell good stories.
- These stories also need sharing with the right audience.

Read

Read and enjoy an article written by Annetta Powell, 5 **Effective Brand Building Strategies to Attract Customers,** *http://www.coxblue.com/5-effective-brand-building-strategies-to-attract-customers-2/*

(70)

4.7 Positioning strategies – company, brand, products and services

"Brand positioning is about finding one unoccupied niche in the prospect's mind, and fill it with something that sticks"
Al Ries & Jack Trout Authors

For entrepreneurs managing existing businesses or planning to enter new markets positioning refers to how you communicate the essential benefits of your business small or large to existing and potential customers. Where you sell your product, how you make it, where you make it and your price all convey subtle messages to the marketplace, even without your using any overt advertising, public relations or promotions. Positioning your business or unique selling proposition is not possible without a plan, it is simple; if you don't know what you stand for and offer how do you expect your customers to know? Positioning strategies could involve many elements of a business from your products and services to your brands, logos and communication. Being strategic in the way that you communicate this to the market creates a position for your business relative to those of competitors. Sending out the wrong message could confuse customers and guide potential customers into the wrong direction. Positioning strategies is one of the most powerful tools in business as it allows you to influence existing and potential customer's perceptions and behaviour deliberately in your favour.

Not having a well-planned and executed positioning strategy allows the opposition to position your offerings in the mind of customers, something you would like to avoid.

Debate

Debate with your teams and stakeholders the status of your overall positioning strategy and verify your understanding with some customer clarification. Also, remember that although businesses have strategies not everyone comply or understand the strategic intend.

- What is your brand positioning strategy?
- Do you have a product positioning strategy? In addition, does it support your brand strategy?
- What is your distribution positioning strategy? Is it supportive of your overall strategy or does it create confusion in the market?

- Do you have a defined price positioning strategy?

There are many more elements in a business's go to market process that contributes to its positioning strategy and it is important that entrepreneurs and business managers have a clear understanding of these drives and its support of the overall positioning strategy.

Watch: Marketing: Positioning, Differentiation, and Value Proposition – YouTube
Watch this short 3:29-minute video by Brain K. McCarthy, **Marketing: Positioning, Differentiation, and Value Proposition,** *http://www.coxblue.com/5-effective-brand-building-strategies-to-attract-customers-2/*

(71)

Do

For all businesses, a positioning strategy defines the tactics, tools and strategies used by a business to differentiate itself from competitors and gain market share. An effective positioning strategy considers the strengths and weaknesses of the business, the needs of the customers and market and the position of competitors. The purpose of a positioning strategy is that it allows a company to spotlight specific areas where they can outshine and beat their competition. Consider some of the suggested strategies below if they are applicable to your business or potential opportunities and what needs to be in place to support the execution of these positioning strategies.
- Cost positioning strategy.
- Quality positioning strategy.
- Flexibility positioning strategy.
- Speed positioning strategy.
- Innovation positioning strategy.

5 - Point plan

Positioning strategies provide internal clarity to entrepreneurs as it focuses activities and drive specific internal behaviours, however the biggest value generated from the market and customers as positioning strategies assist to:

- Communicates consumer wants or satisfaction.
- Communication of characteristic or benefits helps create separation from competitors.
- Could assist with the strong association with individual or group target markets.
- Creates immediate distinction, uniqueness and can provide clear distinction or separation from competitors.
- Generate robust, strong awareness and opportunity for comparisons accentuates characteristics versus competition.

Read

Read and enjoy an article written by Small Business Encyclopaedia, **Positioning,**
https://www.entrepreneur.com/encyclopedia/positioning

(72)

"Positioning in pursuit of your purpose is critical to your success in life. Remember, great strikers are found in the proximity of the penalty box. That is strategic positioning."
Oscar Bimpong

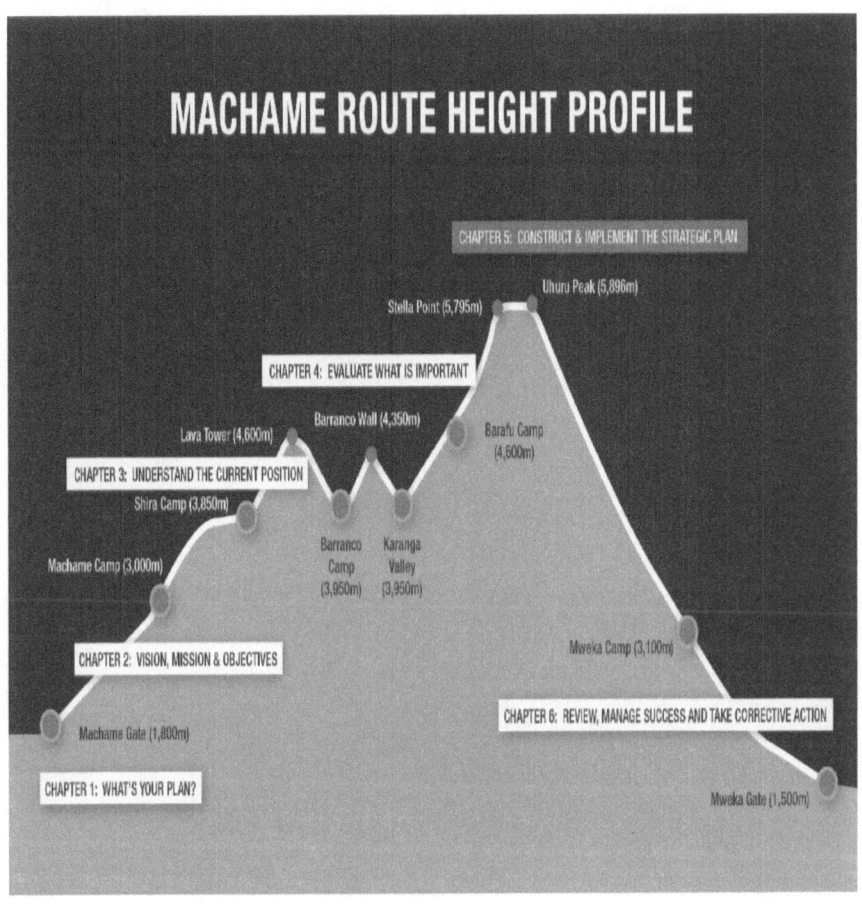

Personal Journey: Barafu Camp – Uhuru Peak
Day 5 on mountain
Barafu Camp – Uhuru Peak (SUMMIT!!) 4,681m (15,358ft) – 5,895m (19,341ft)
Average time to the summit: 7 hours
Uhuru Peak – Mweka Camp (descend) 5,895m (19,341ft) – 3,090m (10,138ft)
Average descending time to Barafu Huts: 3 hours

An early start is required (+/- 11h30pm) for the summit attempt and Uhuru Peak the highest point in Africa at 5,895m. The trail is tougher than anything that you have experienced on your ascent with a sustained switchback climb through steep scree. Slowly and with regular stops is the best way to do it. After Stella Point on the crater rim, it is a very short but very long walk to Uhuru Peak. ***SUMMIT!!!!! The highest peak in Africa****. From the summit it is a sustained descend to Mweka Camp.* **Overnight at Mweka Camp**

Chapter 5: Construct and Implement the strategic plan

"Strategic Planning is a process by which we can envision the future and develop the necessary procedures and operations to influence and achieve that future"
Clark Crouch

5.1 Elements of a strategic plan

The structure of this workbook reflects the key elements for consideration by entrepreneurs during the construction phase of a strategic plan. Entrepreneurs need to: Set the Business Vision, Mission and Objectives, conduct a Macro environmental analysis (external analysis), conduct a Micro environmental analysis (internal analysis), evaluate what is Critical, construct and Implement the strategic plan and also review, manage Successes and take Corrective action.

The detail to all the analysis and considerations needs to be formulated in to a well-structured and strategic plan ready for implementation. It is advisable that strategic plans get saved in a central depository where the relevant stakeholders could have access to the plan however the review and adjustments to the plan needs to be controlled to prevent illegal tampering. Although the master plan should be tamper protected the content of the plan needs to be communicated and shared with all relevant stakeholders for successful implementation. Additional information in strategic plans could also be considered over time as no plan is ever complete and as all plans evolve over time, room should be made for additional considerations.

Debate
Strategic planning is only useful if it becomes the basis for entrepreneurial and management actions. Plans must be alive, plans both long and short term should be made annually. Consider the following as part of your annual planning cycle for existing business

and potential opportunities. Debate with team members and stakeholders the existence of the following planning elements, also allow for updates and reviews:

Elements of a planning system	Yes	No	Next Steps
Have you set a Vision and Mission statement?			
If yes, does it need a review?			
Have you captured your core values?			
If yes, have you communicated it to team members, customers and stakeholders?			
Have you set long-term and short term objectives?			
If yes, do they need to be reviewed?			
What is your strategic agenda (what needs to be done to deliver on the plan)?			
What is the project plan for strategy execution: Metric, Milestones, Accountability			
Have you set the annual budget?			
If yes, does it need to be reviewed?			
Do you have a capital expenditure plan?			
If yes, does it need to be reviewed?			

Watch: What Is the Strategic Planning Process Model Steps Examples Video Lesson Transcript Studycom – YouTube

Watch this short 4:35-minute video by Fernanda Gr, **What Is the Strategic Planning Process Model Steps Examples Video Lesson Transcript Studycom,** *https://www.youtube.com/watch?v=jVRIWeZP52k*

(73)

Do

Asking some key questions regarding the elements considered during the strategic planning process will guide entrepreneurs and business managers to evaluate progress against some actionable

items that will improve the successful development and implementation of strategic business plans:
- Did we complete the analysis required (macro and micro analysis)?
- Did we raise the awareness of the content of our plan amongst stakeholders?
- What is our level of commitment to the plan and have we been able to obtain commitment from some of the key stakeholders to the plan?
- Have we spent enough time planning?
- Are we able to operationalise the set plan?
- Have we made progress with the implementation and have we taken the barriers to implementation into consideration?
- How often do we review our plan?
- Have we spent time on reinforcement of the set plan?

7 - Point plan

While there are numerous elements to the strategic planning process, entrepreneurs need to consider some elements that are key to the success of the plan. It's also interesting to note that none of these have anything to do with the specific contents of the plan:
- Strategic plan timeframe.
- Strategic plan team composition.
- Entrepreneur and or board mandate.
- Don't rush the plan development.
- Focus, focus, focus.
- Address implementation issues head-on.
- Regularly monitor and discuss results.

Read

Read and enjoy an article written by Christoph Sisson, **Key Components of a Winning Strategic Plan,** *http://www.walsworth.com/blog/key-components-winning-strategic-plan*

(74)

"If you don't know where you are going, you are certain to end up somewhere else"
Yogi Berra

5.2 Implementation

The formulation and implementation of a business or marketing plan are in essence two different activities. Understanding the difference is a key ingredient to success. During the implementation process, individuals and businesses take the practical step to do something in relation to the activities suggested by the plan for example: start a promotional program, call on opposition customers, change price points, increase stock holdings and so on. In general, between 65% and 75% of business and marketing plans are unsuccessful and lead to continues frustration amongst entrepreneurs and corporate executives.

The successful implementation of a strategic business plan rest with **YOU! - THE OWNER OR CREATER OF THE PLAN**. Yes, different people action different activities during the implementation process but ultimately the responsibility for the successful implementation remains with you the owner of the plan. Disappointing to note the time and effort individuals and organisations spend on the construction of a plan and then fail with the implementation thereof.

5.2.1 Barriers to effective implementation

As long as a plan remains an idea and don't get implemented successfully it will remain an idea only. Individual entrepreneurs and organisations spend long hours and potentially lots of money developing and formulating strategic business and marketing plans.

These plans simply cannot be allowed to fail due to a lack of implementation. Having a compelling vision and mission should be rewarded by the successful implementation of a strategic business plan that could turn ideas, plans and strategy in to profit? Some of the obstacles faced by entrepreneurs that could lead to strategy implementation failures relate to:
- Lack of internal and external communication.
- Poor leadership.
- Lack of resources to support the implementation process.
- Not everyone is aligned with the objectives of the plan.
- Unrealistic implementation timelines.
- Poor understanding of the external and internal environments.
- Inadequate understanding of competitors and competitor activities.

It is only during the implementation process that the creators of the plan can get feedback of what needs to be adjusted, what is working and what not. Along with the implementation process goes responsibility. The plan needs to be clear on who is responsible for what and by when.

Do

Entrepreneurs and business managers need to review plans from time to time to ensure the plan is still aligned with the business objectives and are actually being implemented.

Doing regular reviews will allow you to take corrective steps and drive behaviours. When reviewing your business or marketing plan, consider the following?
- Do you have a well document plan?
- Do you display leadership with regards to the implementation process?
- Do you communicate effectively concerning the activities of the plan?
- Are you clear with regards to instructions of execution?

- Do you have buy in from team member to assist with the execution process?
- Do you have regular reviews of the progress against plan?
- Have you properly resourced in order to implement the plan?
- Do you understand the macro and micro environments?

Debate

It is important for entrepreneurs and business managers to ensure all functions in a business are aligned with the business plan and ready to support the implementation of the plan.

Debate with interested parties and internal stakeholders whether the steps below have been followed and if not take corrective actions as buy into the plan will greatly support the successful implementation of the plan.

- Was the strategic plan finalised after obtaining input from all invested parties?
- Was the budget aligned to annual goals based on your financial assessment?
- Were the various versions of the plan produced and shared with each internal group?
- Was a scorecard system produced for tracking and monitoring the plan?
- Was a performance management and reward system produced and implemented?
- Was the plan rolled out to the whole organisation?
- Were the entire department's annual plans built around the corporate plan?
- Was monthly strategy meetings set up with established reporting to monitor your progress?
- Were annual strategic review dates set up, including new assessments and a large group meeting for an annual plan review?

Watch:  The Secret to Strategic Implementation – YouTube

Watch this short 3:29-minute video by Erica Olsen, **The Secret to Strategic Implementation,**
https://www.youtube.com/watch?v=ndCexCPLNdA

(75)

8 - Point plan

It is interesting that often the creators of a strategic plan are surprised if the plan is not implemented and performing as expected and not understanding the reasons for poor performance.

To avoid these surprises and misunderstandings take a moment to honestly answer the following questions:
- How committed are you to implementing the plan to move your company forward?
- How do you plan to communicate the plan through the company?
- Are there sufficient people who have bought in to the plan to drive it forward?
- How are you going to motivate your people?
- Have you identified internal processes that are key to driving the plan forward?
- Are you going to commit capital, resources, and time to support the plan?
- What are the roadblocks to implementing and supporting the plan?
- How will you take available resources and achieve maximum results with them?

Read

Read and enjoy an article written by TCCii Strategic and Management Consultants, **Implementing A Strategic Plan Successfully,**
http://www.mondaq.com/x/140370/Operational+Performance+Management/Implementing+A+Strategic+Plan+Successfully

(76)

"Weak leadership can wreck the soundest strategy"
Sun Tzu

5.2.2 Successful plan implementation

Being successful has many different connotation's and interpretations to different people, however successful strategic business or marketing plan implementation simply means - have you achieved what you set out to achieve given the strategic plan set objectives? If not, the level of success will always be questionable. It is the responsibility of the owner of the plan; entrepreneur or executive to ensure the strategic plan is successfully implemented. The rewards of a successful plan implementation should contribute to an increase in sales revenue, profit and potentially an increase in market share.

Successful plan implementation could also support the maintenance of a company's current position as long as it's in line with the plan objectives.

Debate

The successful implementation of a strategic plan could be enhanced by debating the answers to some of the questions posed below and ensuring actions are taken by entrepreneurs and business managers in association with team members to monitor and adapt behaviours to drive the successful implementation of the strategic plan.

- Are your initiatives aligned?
- What level of successful strategic business or marketing plan implementation is important for you in your business?
- Are your budgets and performances aligned?
- What are your values and expectations?
- Are you following the principal of structure follow strategy?
- Who needs to take responsibility for the successful implementation of your business plan?
- Did you engage with your staff?
- What measures would you implement to gauge the success of your plan?
- Have you suggested some corrective actions that need to be taken if any?

Watch: Business Plan Implementation - YouTube

Watch this short 2:51-minute video by Florida Buy and Sell Business Brokers, **Business Plan Implementation,**
https://www.youtube.com/watch?v=jjxG2-m436Y

(77)

Do

Implementing your strategic plan would be one of the most important activities undertaken by entrepreneurs and business owners hoping to grow their businesses and unlock new opportunities. Once you are confident you have a thorough, comprehensive strategic plan for your business, you can take steps to implement the actions outlined in the plan. The implementation of a plan is more likely to succeed if you have adequate resources and expertise to implement it. If you or your team do not know how to implement your business' strategic plan, seek direction and advice from experts and the skills of your personnel. Below are suggested steps and actions that could assist with the successful implementation of your plan:

- Communicate with your team members and extended staff.
- Know your end goal.
- Monitor your progress.
- Develop contingency plans.
- Seek expert advice.

7 - Point plan

The success of a strategic plan implementation starts during the construction phase of the plan and entrepreneurs need to support this process making use of a "dashboard" with key metrics to assist in the monitoring, implementation and results generation of the plan.

- Clarify the time frame selected for the strategic plan.
- Make sure you select the individual or team responsible for the construction of the strategic plan wisely.
- Ensure the mandate given for the construction of the strategic plan is clear.
- Allow adequate time for the development of the plan.
- Keep the strategic plan very focused.
- Ensure you address the implementation process during the plan development phase.
- Regularly monitor and discuss the implementation of the plan.

Read

Read and enjoy an article written by Laura Click, **8 Important Steps to Successfully Implement Your Marketing Plan,**
https://flybluekite.com/how-to-implement-your-marketing-plan/

(78)

5.2.3 Methods to improve strategy implementation

It is important that the owner of the plan "entrepreneurs or executives" understand the content of the plan and ensure all stakeholders were consulted. Stakeholders will be critical during the formulation of the strategic plan but become even more critical during the execution process. Keep stakeholders informed and make them part of the celebration process when progress is shown. Leaders need to lead with authority, determination and focus.

If you are the leader responsible for strategy implementation ensure you communicate to team members the importance of the plan, the objectives and timelines and most off all make sure each individual has a clear understanding of what is expected of them in order to deliver on the plan; particularly about what is acceptable and what is not acceptable.

Do not expect miracles if you have not properly resourced the organisation in order to deliver on a strategic plan – for example if you need additional sales people to cover new geographical areas in line with your strategy – appoint them. Strategic plans give direction but during implementation you might have to make some tactical (day-to-day adjustments) changes. Good leaders can only do that if they are actively involved in the implementation process – get involved. If it is important to you it will be important to your team.

Debate

Entrepreneurs and business managers could improve the implementation of strategic business plans by debating the response to some of the questions below and if the experience is negative take corrective actions to remedy the situation. The characteristics of an effective strategic plan implementation are reflected below:

- The strategic plan must communicate the selected strategy,
- it must measure performance in real time, and
- it must offer integrated plan management capability, and
- it must acknowledge and enable emotional contracting with all staff, which is so vital for linking individual commitment and activity to the attainment of organisational plans.

Watch:  Strategic Planning: Three Keys to Successful Execution - YouTube

Watch this 53:52-minute video by Denise Harrison, **Strategic Planning: Three Keys to Successful Execution,**
https://www.youtube.com/watch?v=-CxXQbVMYOM

(79)

Do

Like all things in life we could develop better and proposed ways of implementing activities and thought processes. This is no different for strategic plan implementation. Entrepreneurs and business managers would be well equipped considering the suggestions below in order to improve the effectiveness of selected strategic plan implementation:

- Translate the strategy into specific strategic objectives (for each unit and or department).

- Create specific clarity around your organisation's leading goals. For instance, within your "Customer Objectives" the goal may be to "grow sales":
    - Management consensus – management must know *how* it will grow sales before your team will know how to achieve this goal.
    - Identify measures that indicate how to track progress.
    - Identify targets that quantify the measure.
    - Establish deadlines for achieving incremental target goals.
- Communicate the goal, educate and inform your people about this goal.
- Work with your team to define and regularly measure and refine the activities required to achieve deadline driven goals and targets.
- Identify resources, people and processes that need to be linked, developed or refined to support goal achievement.
- Provide consistent, regular reviews, feedback and learning.

5 - Point plan

In order to improve the success rate of strategic plan implementation entrepreneurs and business managers need to follow activities of continuous improvement. Below are some basic principles that could lead to a higher level of successful implementation. Entrepreneurs needs to display leadership that embraces top-down direction and upward influence, supported with a clear strategy and priorities.

- Constructive conflict leading to a common voice needs to be implemented with open communication.

- Effective coordination should support the implementation process.

- Down-the-line leadership with clear accountability and authority needs to be part of the business structure.

- Strategic plan implementation training needs to be made available to team members.

Read

Read and enjoy an article written by Makrand Dekhane, **Strategy Implementation – Challenges,** *https://www.linkedin.com/pulse/20141210074437-19753552-strategy-implementation-challenges*

(80)

> *"The essence of strategy is choosing what not to do."*
> **Michael Porter**

5.3 Control

Control is one of the most important elements effecting the successful implementation of any plan or strategy. Entrepreneurs and business managers alike will agree, without control you are not able to manage or influence effectively. In business as in life people often say: tell me how you measure me and I will show you how I behave. Without control entrepreneurs are not able to manage effectively and will find it difficult to review, project and take corrective actions. Having control over the implementation of a strategic plan simply means you are in a position to understand what needs to be done to correct actions or activities that are not being executed according to the plan but more important you can instruct or influence corrective actions.

Taking action timeously could be the difference between good or bad plan implementation. In order to take control entrepreneurs, need indicators to guide and reflect on the current status of the plan implementation.

This often takes the shape of a strategic plan "dashboard" with variables that indicate progress against set plan objectives and actions. The dashboard needs to be reflective of the key drivers for the strategic plan with set objectives and timelines. Plans are not implemented in isolation and seldom by the creator of the plan.

Entrepreneurs and business managers implement through people. Thus control and corrective actions almost always include people. Controlling plan implementation also relies on entrepreneur's motivation, managerial and people skills. This will include motivational activities and management control that could be perceived as harsh but without praise and strict management plans will not stay on course. Having no control will waste time and money.

Debate
Regularly review and discuss with your teams and stakeholders some of the control elements below in order to measure and gauge strategic plan implementation based on specific control elements. Once done decide if corrective action needs to be taken, be mindful of timelines and expectations. Consider the suggested control variables below:

Control variables for plan implementation	Yes	No	Corrective Action
Positive customer feedback			
Positive and significant movement in target market sales			
Positive performance against budgets			
Positive movement in market share			
Regular competitor analysis			
Regular cost analysis			

Watch: Balanced Scorecard - YouTube

Watch this short 3:59-minute video by Intrafocus as one of the monitoring elements that could lead to better control and the taking of timeous corrective actions, **Balanced Scorecard,** *https://www.youtube.com/watch?v=M_IlOlywryw&list=PLMYJuXb3F_KsOWLpYgctR2BM1yHUgu-JP*

(81)

Do

In moving from a current position to a newly nominated position it is natural that entrepreneurs and business managers will monitor progress, however entrepreneurs will agree that monitoring without control amounts to no progress. In order to control strategic plan implementation some processes and procedures need to be in place or developed. See some suggestions below:

- Set performance standards, if standards are not achieved take corrective action.
- Construct weekly, monthly and quarterly checklists, if these checklists are not ticked take corrective action (it is part of control).
- Measure responses to your plan implementation, if the responses are negative initiate tactics to improve the outputs.
- Continuously compare your results against the standards you set and the plan objectives.

5 - Point plan

Controls are necessary for the evaluation phase. Controls established during the creation of the marketing plan provide benchmarks to assess how well the plan accomplished its goals.

Controls are like goals; they give the entrepreneur something to aim for when enacting the plan. Controls may include measures such as the marketing budgets and market share.

- During the implementation process of any strategic plan entrepreneurs will always have a need for feedback, appraisals and reward.
- Controls need to be in place to check and validate strategic choices.
- Congruence between decisions and intended strategy need to be evaluated and corrective actions taken if deviations are found.
- Controls and actions will lead to the improvement of existing plans and the creation of new ones.

Read

Read and enjoy an article written by Dr Omar Hasan Kasule, **0807- Planning, Implementation, Control, and Evaluation,** *http://omarkasule-05.tripod.com/id329.html*

(82)

"Control your own destiny or someone else will"
Jack Welch

So What's your Plan?

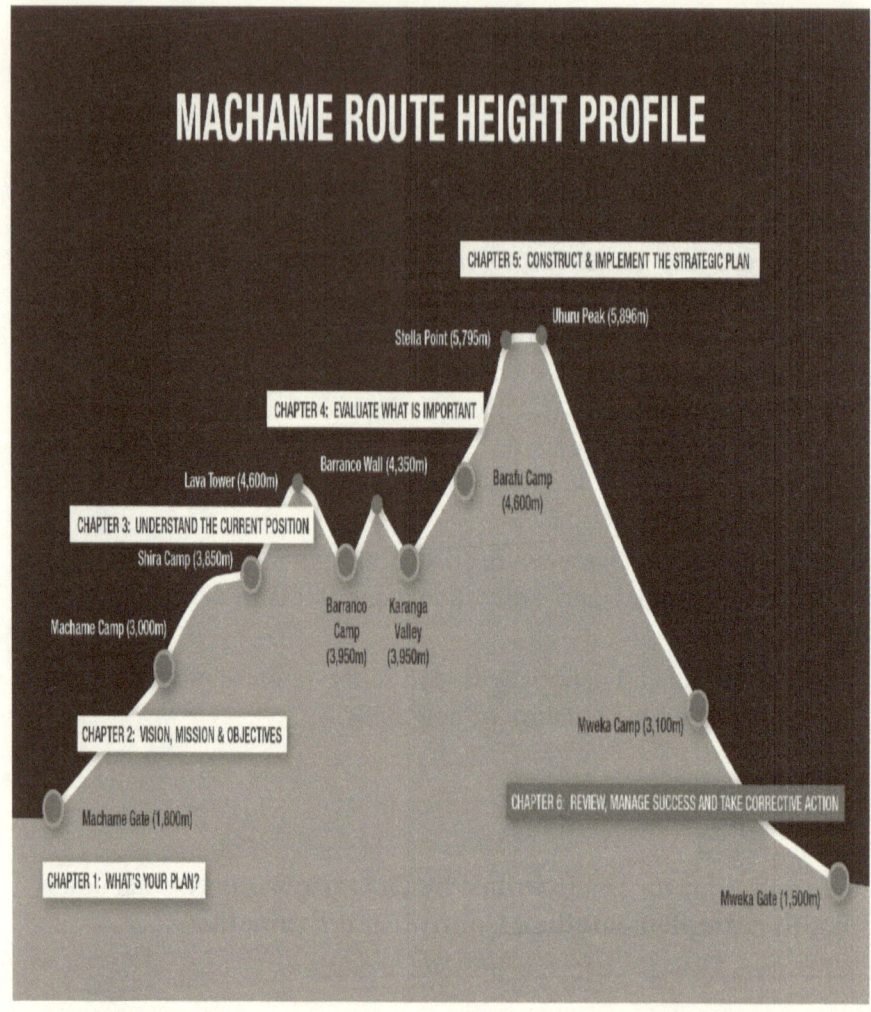

Personal Journey: Mweka Camp – Mweka Gate

After Stella Point on the crater rim, it is a very short but very long walk to Uhuru Peak. **SUMMIT!!!!! The highest peak in Africa**

Day 6 on mountain
Mweka Camp – Mweka Gate 3,090m (10,138ft) – 1,641m (5,384ft)
Average hiking time: 4 hours
The day is spent descending through open moorlands and the rain forest to the Park Gate. Transfer to a heavenly shower and a real bed at the RIGHT altitude.

"Organizations are most vulnerable when they are at the peak of their success"
R. T. Lenz

Chapter 6: Review, manage successes and take corrective action

"There is going to be a detailed review, an investigation, if you will, of the incident. We will look at how the plan was executed and lessons we've learned from that"
Paul Wattles

6.1 Review for results

The final step in any planning process is to review, monitor and evaluate progress against the set plan. During the construction phase of the plan entrepreneurs and team members would have decided on the frequency of the plan review, what will be reviewed and who needs to be involved. All plans have milestones and indicators that will provide a dashboard of important information to check that development is on track. The things you decide to measure will give an indication of how well you are doing. When reviewing progress towards achieving the plans, strategic aims and objectives, entrepreneurs and business managers need to ensure the activities are kept within the parameters of the agreed objectives, they are consistent with the organisations vision, mission and values. Entrepreneurs also need to continuously review internal and external changes which may require adjustments to the organisation's strategy or affect its ability to achieve their objectives.

Once you have completed your strategic plan you might ask how often should you go back and look at it to determine if the plan is still valid (heading in the right direction) and staying on the course you have chosen? Its common practise to revisit your plan and the assumptions you made while developing the strategic plan at least once a quarter, as well as revisiting the entire plan annually. Entrepreneurs and business managers might ask; Why? Logically your strategic plan is based on your knowledge of your business, your business conditions, or environment, and the assumptions you and your team have made about what will happen in the operating environment.

6.2 Manage for success

Despite the hours invested in developing strategic plans, all too often they don't work. Entrepreneurs and business managers are the owners of these plans and need to ensure they manage the implementation and continue execution of these plans. Managing strategic plans means high levels of communications with stakeholders, the vision, mission and objectives needs to be communicated to all who are expected to deliver on the plan. Every tactical action supporting the strategic objectives needs to be included in an overall communication plan so that the strategy is reinforced. Every member of the implementation and execution team needs to understand their role in the success of the plan. The successful management of a strategic plan requires leadership from the entrepreneur, business manager and all who are involved with the plan formulation and execution. Poor or weak leadership leads to improper resource allocation, lack of buy-in, poor follow-through, inadequate checks, misaligned goals, -strategies, -actions, inefficient rewards and punishments, cover-ups and many more. It is simple: the plan needs leadership. Proper management of a strategic plan implies you have a plan to manage, make sure the plan has substance based on the analysis done. Ensure your plan is not just a great idea. Labelling something a strategic plan or initiative does not make it one.

You should be able to break down your strategic plan in double actions so that team members who need to deliver on these actions understand how it applies to them and what it is they need to do and by when. When we manage a strategic plan we could select to either manage it properly or not at all - avoid passive management. Do not assume things will run themselves after we get them started. Failing to assign and hold individuals accountable for delivering on the assignments leads to poor management: all talk and no action. Lead from the font, be involved and hold people accountable. Management of the strategic plan without taking personal ownership and motivating others is just not possible.

When leaders take ownership of the management process of strategic plans they should be able to explain to others what is in it for them. People should also be able to find meaning in what they do. People want to build something and make a difference, if they don't understand the purpose, goals are undermined and the vision disappears. Entrepreneurs need to build confidence with team members by making sure they understand the importance of their contribution to the strategic plan by celebrating successes. Incentive schemes and personal recognition will go a long way in managing strategic plans with success.

> *"Leadership is a matter of having people look at you and gain confidence...If you're in control, they're in control"*
> **Tom Landry, Head Coach Dallas Cowboys (1960-88)**

6.3 Celebrate your successes

It is important that entrepreneurs and business managers along with their team members all step back from time to time and acknowledge your progress and celebrate your successes, both small and large. It is important to celebrate your successes, celebrate completion of the strategic-planning and goal-setting process, celebrate achievement of key goals and celebrate when the team receives special recognition. Reward good effort. Suggested ways your team can celebrate success:

- Certificates, silly gifts, tickets to games or shows.
- Chart progress in a public area.
- Give praise in front of pears.
- Have a goals-achieved section of the rewards agenda to give these extra recognitions.
- Looking for opportunities to nominate your team for an appropriate award.
- Share cake, ice cream or provide a meal before a meeting. Or just invite the team to come together for a social without a formal meeting.
- Recognise the accomplishments of specific members of the team in front of the team members.

- Recognise the team in your local newsletter.
- Send a thank-you note.
- Share your team successes with others in the industry
- Start the meeting by recognizing special accomplishments since the previous meeting

Often we see leaders use intentional celebration of success to bring focus and team alignment. Celebrations remind team members of the importance of their strategic work in situations where the team focus is easily drawn away from company goals by competing demands of the day-to-day workplace. Leaders also use celebration to maintain momentum through a prolonged and difficult change initiative. In either case, celebration demonstrates management's satisfaction with outcomes and effort. Recognising and appreciating good results inevitably leads to greater focus on what matters. Morale and productivity improves. Success breeds success.

> *"Celebrate what you want to see more of"*
> **Tom Peters**

6.4 Taking corrective action

> *"Wisdom comes from life experience; life experience is the result of repeatedly taking corrective action while courageously learning from mistakes"*
> **Ken Poirot**

With reference to strategic plans and the plan implementation, taking corrective action is critical to ensure the plan stays on course and objectives are achieved. It is the responsibility of the owner of the plan (entrepreneur or business manager) to identify obstacles, decide on what needs to be done and instructing corrective actions. Obstacles to plan execution could be plentiful and complex ranging from changing conditions internal and or externally that might also call for a change in day-to-day tactical deviations. Taking corrective actions timeously could influence the success of your selected strategic plan.

Debate

Taking corrective action is one of the three essential elements of the control process. If the results of the control process don't meet company set standards, then it needs to be revamped to meet organisational set goals.

Debate with team members your current process for taking corrective actions by considering the suggested process below:
- Managers need to understand the contributing factors of a problem and how it impacts key processes; they must then figure out a workable solution.
- The first step in the problem-solving process is identifying the problem, which can be hard to distinguish from symptoms of the problem.
- Once the problem is identified, the entrepreneur or business manager must decide what corrective action to take. In many ways, identifying and solving a problem (the control process) is a process, not a once-off event.
- Organisations may decide to discuss a problem and potential solutions with stakeholders before taking corrective actions.

Watch: 10 Strategic Management: Strategy Evaluation and Control - YouTube
Watch this interesting 10:22-minute video by Executive Finance, **10 Strategic Management: Strategy Evaluation and Control,** *https://www.youtube.com/watch?v=NfKLoGZiR4s*

So What's your Plan?

(83)

Do 👆

During the implementation and execution phase of strategic plans corrective action is the term used to refer to a set of actions to resolve a threat to the plan's constraints or a defect in its structure. In other words, these are the actions taken by the plan owner (entrepreneur or business manager) to deal with anything that can influence the project in a negative manner. In taking corrective action, the objective is to select and implement actions that will resolve deviations from the plan. Corrective action can be triggered during monitoring and measurement activities.

If the plan progress is not checked on a regular basis, there is a danger that it will get out of control. In order to make informed decisions and exercise rational control, it is necessary to compare what has actually happened with what was expected to happen and what might happen next (including any risks and concerns).

The objective of this activity is to maintain an accurate and current picture of progress on the work being carried out and the status of its resources. Now that this stage has been completed, it is worth reflecting on the key points of the control and execution phase supported by corrective actions. Consider the checklist below that will assist in clearly identifying problem areas that warrant corrective actions:
- Develop and manage your strategic plan at a detailed level.
- Have regular team meetings to discuss progress and concerns.
- Address concerns in a timely manner and listen for suggestions.

- Make sensible decisions based on well-documented analysis options.
- Provide well-documented status reports on progress and issues.
- Take corrective action and ensure it is implemented.

5 - Point plan

For entrepreneurs and business managers to manage risks associated with strategic plans requires tracking progress and taking potential corrective actions that might include:
- Identifying the reason for being off-track and taking the appropriate action when off-track.
- Rigorously checking that implementation is not at fault.
- Revising the analysis using updated values when change is implemented correctly.
- Re-examining the original analyses when the original projections are not on-track. Using your own information can add confidence to the review.
- Re-examining the strategy regularly, or in the event of a new opportunity weekly.

Read

Read and enjoy an article written by Michael Mankins and Richard Steele, **Turning Great Strategy into Great Performance,** *https://hbr.org/2005/07/turning-great-strategy-into-great-performance*

(84)

"If you know the enemy and know yourself, you need not fear the results of a hundred battles. If you know yourself but not the enemy, for every victory gained you will also suffer a defeat. If you know neither the enemy nor yourself, you will succumb in every battle"
Sun Tsu

Recommended Readings and Viewing – QR Codes

 **(1) Watch:** **Is a Business Plan Any Use? – YouTube**
If you had any doubts regarding the value of having a plan watch this 6-minute video from Cranfield University's School of Management, **Is a Business Plan Any Use?**
https://www.youtube.com/watch?v=3jK25e8cJA4

 **(2) Read**
Read and enjoy an article written by Mark Henricks "Do You Really Need a Business Plan? "
https://www.entrepreneur.com/article/198618

(3) Watch: **How-to Write a Great Business Vision Statement - YouTube**
If you have difficulties writing a great business vision statement watch this 5-minute video from Dr Susan L. Reid, **How-to Write a Great Business Vision Statement,**
https://www.youtube.com/watch?v=Jtz05G1B4i8

 **(3B) Read**

12 Truly Inspiring Company Vision and Mission Statement Examples, By Lindsay Kolowich,
https://blog.hubspot.com/marketing/inspiring-company-mission-statements#sm.0001772c5ke6tcymw6s14mzfaqv3x

 **(4) Watch:** How to Write a Mission Statement – YouTube

If you need some inspiration to write your mission statements watch this short 5-minute video by Erica Olsen, **How to Write a Mission Statement,** *https://www.youtube.com/watch?v=XtyCt83JLNY*

 **(5) Read**

Read and enjoy an article written by **Nicole Fallon, What is a Mission Statement?** *https://www.businessnewsdaily.com/3783-mission-statement.html*

 **(6) Watch:** Setting Objectives - Video 1 and 2 - YouTube

If you need some inspiration to formulate and to write your personal and or business objectives watch this short 3-minute video by David Bozward, **Setting Objectives,** *https://www.youtube.com/watch?v=hD9gaqZ94UQ*

 **(7) Watch:** **Setting Objectives - Video 1 and 2 – YouTube**

For more specific business objective setting watch this 16-minute video by Geoff Riley,
https://www.youtube.com/watch?v=KxjbQ3otNIE

 **(8) Read**

Read and enjoy an article written by George N Root III, **10 Most Important Business Objectives,**
http://smallbusiness.chron.com/10-important-business-objectives-23686.html

 **(9) Watch:** **Overcome Obstacles and Challenges to Achieve a Goal - YouTube**

Overcoming barriers to achieve objectives and more specific business plan objectives watch this short 5-minute video by Stephen Goldberg **Overcome Obstacles and Challenges to Achieve a Goal,**
https://www.youtube.com/watch?v=uuWhqzJLFF8

 **(10) Read**

Read and enjoy an article written by Kay Fudala, How **to Overcome Barriers To Achieving Goals,** *http://redgramliving.com/2013/08/20/how-to-overcome-barriers-to-achieving-goals/*

 (11) Watch: Environmental scanning - YouTube

Watch this short 4.5-minute video by Teo Hiro, **How internal and External Factors Drive Organizational Change** to obtain a better understanding of environmental scanning and its benefits to an organisation, *https://www.youtube.com/watch?v=Kt6J-jCcdXk*

 (12) Read

Read and enjoy an article written by Vibhav Srivastava, **Importance of Understanding Business Environment,** *http://in.viadeo.com/en/groups/detaildiscussion/?containerId=0021 t7mup2amy1o5&forumId=00218vlbvywso7e3&action=messageDet ail&messageId=0025811ykdrvs0y*

 (13) Watch: Macro Environmental Forces - YouTube

Watch this short 4.5-minute video by Art Mollengarden, **Macro Environmental Forces,** *https://www.youtube.com/watch?v=lgzeSkil1SE*

173

So What's your Plan?

 **(14) Read**
Read and enjoy an article written by Jim Tischler, **Macro environmental Forces Affecting Marketing,**
http://smallbusiness.chron.com/macroenvironmental-forces-affecting-marketing-71632.html

 **(15) Watch:** **How to review business economic factors – YouTube**
Watch this short 4.5-minute video by Terry Rachwalski, **How to review business economic factors,**
https://www.youtube.com/watch?v=mz5D7FFGptM

 **(16) Read**
Read and enjoy an article written by Anders Borg, **6 Factors shaping the global economy in 2016,**
https://www.weforum.org/agenda/.../6-factors-shaping-the-global-economy-in-2016/

 **(17) Watch:** **Main influences: Government policies | Business Studies ... - YouTube**
Watch this short 2.5-minute video by Moira Millard, **Main influences: Government policies | Business,**
https://www.youtube.com/watch?v=lTx9Z5rDYUQ

So What's your Plan?

 **(18) Read**

Read and enjoy an article written by Joynal Abdin, **Impact of government policies on business,**
https://www.linkedin.com/pulse/impact-government-policies-business-md-joynal-abdin

 **(19) Watch:** **Back to The Future - Technology and the Four Big Trends that will impact the next 15 years - YouTube**

Watch this short 16:30-minute video by Daniel Priestley, **Back To The Future - Technology and the Four Big Trends that will impact the next 15 years,**
https://www.youtube.com/watch?v=yEZcsgA4JsQ

 **(20) Read**

Read and enjoy an article written by Alex Pirouz, **The Impact of Technology in Business,**
www.businessreviewaustralia.com/technology/.../The-Impact-of-Technology-in-Busin.

 **(21) Watch:** **5 Legal Basics Entrepreneurs Need to Know - YouTube**

Watch this short 16:30-minute video by Merissa V Grayson , **5 Legal Basics Entrepreneurs Need to Know,** *https://www.youtube.com/watch?v=TpEwgbgzeMc*

 **(22) Read**
Read and enjoy an article written by Chad Brooks, **9 Regulatory Issues That Will Affect Small Business,** *http://www.businessnewsdaily.com/5673-small-business-laws-in 2014.html#sthash.uabzKbfD.dpuf*

 **(23) Watch:** **The Social Environment and Cultural Environment – YouTube** Watch this short 5:54-minute video by Alanis Business Academy, **The Social Environment,** *https://www.youtube.com/watch?v=rXty8_fMjk4*

 **(24) Watch:** **The Social Environment and Cultural Environment – YouTube**
also watch this short 2:17-minutes video by B2Bwhiteboard , **Cultural Environment,**
https://www.youtube.com/watch?v=2M0GDRhS0MA

 **(25) Read**

Read and enjoy an article written by Joseph Zammit-Lucia, **Businesses cannot avoid involvement in cultural, social and moral issues,** *https://www.theguardian.com/sustainable-business/business-confront-cultural-social-moral-issues*

 **(26) Watch:** **How Do Business Affect the Environment? – YouTube**
Watch this short 1:19-minute video by Coleen Go, **How Do Business Affect the Environment?**
https://www.youtube.com/watch?v=PdgNHVpOsUM

 **(27) Read**
Read and enjoy an article written by Anup Shah, **Corporations and the Environment,**
http://www.globalissues.org/article/55/corporations-and-the-environment

 **(28) Watch:** **Marketing Briefs TV: Internal Business Analysis – YouTube** Watch this short 15:42-minute video by Tony Marino, Marketing Briefs TV: Internal Business Analysis,
https://www.youtube.com/watch?v=1OEHyDBNrWM

 **(29) Read**
Read and enjoy an article written by Subho Mukher jee, **7 Factors Determining the Internal Environment of a Business,** *http://www.economicsdiscussion.net/business-environment/7-factors-determining-the-internal-environment-of-a-business/10099*

 **(30) Watch:** **Industry Analysis – YouTube**
Watch this short 6.29-minute video by Corporate Bridge, **Industry Analysis,** *https://www.youtube.com/watch?v=C8rUL4q8evw*

 **(31) Read**
Read and enjoy an article written by Shanmukha Rao. Padala and Dr. N. V.S. Suryanarayana, **Industry Analysis,** *http://www.articlesbase.com/industrial-articles/industry-analysis-3187078.html*

 **(32) Watch:** **Understanding Customer Needs – YouTube**
Watch this short 2.10-minute video by Infoteam Sales Process Consulting, **Understanding Customer Needs,** *https://www.youtube.com/watch?v=2C-2v99paQM*

So What's your Plan?

 **(33) Read**
Read and enjoy an article written by Ross Beard, **Why Customer Satisfaction is Important (6 Reasons),**
http://blog.clientheartbeat.com/why-customer-satisfaction-is-important/

 **(34) Watch:** **Supplier selection - YouTube**
Watch this short 3.15-minute video by SarabandaFashion, **Supplier selection,** *https://www.youtube.com/watch?v=mjWBjw5f0wM*

 **(35) Read**
Read and enjoy an article written by Brad Egeland, **Choosing a Vendor: Six Steps to Find the Best Supplier,**
http://www.businessknowhow.com/manage/choosevendor.htm

 **(36) Watch:** **Understanding Your Competition – YouTube**
Watch this short 7:39-minute video by Nial Strickland, **Understanding Your Competition,**
https://www.youtube.com/watch?v=NEfSyDSaXXk

 **(37) Read**

Read and enjoy an article written by Tim Berry, **Know Your Competition,** *https://www.entrepreneur.com/article/78596*

 **(38) Watch:** **What are distribution channels? YouTube**

Watch this short 7:39-minute video by LearnLoads, **What are distribution channels?**
https://www.youtube.com/watch?v=JfBbSLaj0Pc

 **(39) Read**

Read and enjoy an article written by Tony Robbins, **DISTRIBUTION CHANNELS,**
http://www.referenceforbusiness.com/small/Di-Eq/Distribution-Channels.html

 **(40) Watch:** **The Employees First, Customers Second Transformation Journey, YouTube**

Watch this short 7:13-minute video by HCL Technologies, **The Employees First, Customers Second Transformation Journey,**
https://www.youtube.com/watch?v=HmV9dmG1XdY

So What's your Plan?

 **(41) Read**

Read and enjoy an article written by Rita Trehan, **The Importance of Finding the Right Talent,** *https://www.linkedin.com/pulse/importance-finding-right-talent-rita-trehan*

 **(42) Watch:** **Social Media Marketing -- How It Affects Your Business – YouTube**

Watch this short 4:25-minute video by, SbrTechnologies Biswajit Singh, **Social Media Marketing -- How it Affects Your Business – YouTube,** *https://www.youtube.com/watch?v=yDA864UskXc*

 **(43) Read**

Read and enjoy an article written by Timothy Sykes, **8 Tips to Grow Your Business Using Social Media,** *https://www.entrepreneur.com/article/278598*

 **(44) Watch:** **What is Stakeholder Engagement? - YouTube**

Watch this short 3:07-minute video by Future 500, **What is Stakeholder Engagement?** *https://www.youtube.com/watch?v=VHGTsEwbOJY*

So What's your Plan?

 (45) Read

Read and enjoy an article written by John Friedman, **Stakeholder Relationships: Key to a Sustainable Enterprise,**
https://www.google.com/url?sa=t&rct=j&q=&esrc=s&source=web&cd=&cad=rja&uact=8&ved=0ahUKEwiwwKjOg93RAhXKD8AKHRfhAlQQFggqMAI&url=http%3A%2F%2Fwww.huffingtonpost.com%2Fjohn-friedman%2Fmanaging-stakeholder-rela_b_1415255.html&usg=AFQjCNGgpPN8cys8zqPJYNp4lZKpIKXH0A

 (46) Watch: What Is Corporate Culture? - YouTube

Watch this short 2:30-minute video by Strategyandbusiness, **What Is Corporate Culture?**
https://www.youtube.com/watch?v=gficoigz1xs

 (47) Read

Read and enjoy an article written by Michaek Essany, **6 Ways to Build a Great Corporate Culture for Your Small Business,**
http://quickbooks.intuit.com/r/employees/6-ways-to-build-a-great-corporate-culture-for-your-small-business/

So What's your Plan?

 **(48) Watch:** **Launching a start-up - Key Resources - YouTube**
Watch this short 4:45-minute video by Aamar Aslam, **Launching a start-up - Key Resources**, *https://www.youtube.com/watch?v=oNo2SCHmrIE*

 **(49) Read**
Read and enjoy a post written by David Ehrenberg, **What is the best way to identify the financial, human and physical resource requirements for a business?** *https://www.quora.com/What-is-the-best-way-to-identify-the-financial-human-and-ph*.

 **(50) Watch:** **Market analysis - YouTube**
Watch this short 20:00-minute video by Henning Glaser, **Market analysis,** *https://www.youtube.com/watch?v=g5rVxlLPAF8*

 **(51) Read**
Read and enjoy a post written by Joy Levin, **How Marketing Research Can Benefit a Small Business,** *https://smallbiztrends.com/2006/01/how-marketing-research-can-benefit-a-small-business.html*

183

So What's your Plan?

 **(52) Watch:** **Understanding Customer Needs – YouTube**
Watch this 44:35-minute video by Galton College, **Customer Analysis,** *https://www.youtube.com/watch?v=v5M4HZRVDJI*

 **(53) Read**
Read and enjoy a post written by Jesamine, **Customer Analysis: How to Effectively Target the Market,**
https://blog.udemy.com/customer-analysis/

 **(54) Watch:** **Understanding Your Competition – YouTube** Watch this short 5:48-minute video by D2D Millionaire, **Do you know your competition?**
https://www.youtube.com/watch?v=ROkCX_8YRww

 **(55) Watch:** **Putting Your SWOT to Work - YouTube**
Watch this short 3:46-minute video by Elsa Ozuna Richards, **Putting Your SWOT to Work,**
https://www.youtube.com/watch?v=exm9uAKYkl0

 **(56) Read**

Read and enjoy an article written by Julia Padget, **What is SWOT analysis and how can it add value?**

https://www.linkedin.com/pulse/what-swot-analysis-how-can-add-value-julia

 **(57) Watch:** **Strategic Plan Review – Cowlitz County - YouTube**

Watch this short 8:49-minute video by Kevin Hunter, **Strategic Plan Review – Cowlitz County,**

https://www.youtube.com/watch?v=SGtLEWTzimc

 **(58) Read**

Read and enjoy an article written by Rich Horwath, **5 Critical Moments to Evaluate Your Strategy,**

http://www.skipprichard.com/5-critical-moments-to-evaluate-your-strategy/

 **(59) Watch:** **How to Identify Target Market | Target Market Examples -YouTube**

Watch this short 7:00-minute video by Network Marketing Success, **How to Identify Target Market | Target Market Examples,**

https://www.youtube.com/watch?v=hE5z7essD7E

 **(60) Read**

Read and enjoy an article written by April Dunford, **Start-up Market Segmentation: 5 Steps to Selecting a Target Market,** *http://www.rocketwatcher.com/blog/2015/04/startup-market-segmentation.html*

 **(61) Watch:**  **How to Develop Competitive Advantage - YouTube**

Watch this short 3:31-minute video by Erica Olsen, **How to Develop Competitive Advantage,** *https://www.youtube.com/watch?v=S9O2oPbT3fs*

 **(62) Read**

Read and enjoy an article written by Peter Voogd, **5 Ways Entrepreneurs Can Gain a Competitive Advantage,** *https://www.entrepreneur.com/article/243717*

 **(63) Watch:** **The Product Life Cycle - YouTube**

Watch this short 6:34-minute video by Alanis Business Academy, **The Product Life Cycle,** *https://www.youtube.com/watch?v=KVMTMfCO1dY*

 **(64) Read**

Read and enjoy an article written by Note Desk, **Product Life Cycle (PLC)**, *http://www.notesdesk.com/notes/marketing/product-life-cycle-plc/*

 **(65) Watch:**  **Introduction to stakeholder maps - YouTube**

Watch this short 4:55-minute video by LearnLoads, **Introduction to stakeholder maps,**
https://www.youtube.com/watch?v=bOIT1GKVMd8

 **(66) Read**

Read and enjoy an article written by Deborah Shane, **11 Ways to Build Solid, Strong, Lasting Business Relationships,**
https://smallbiztrends.com/2015/06/build-lasting-business-relationships.html

 **(67) Watch:**  **Competitive Strategy in 3 Minutes - YouTube**

Watch this short 3:29-minute video by Prof Joe Urbany, **Competitive Strategy in 3 Minutes,**
https://www.youtube.com/watch?v=bl5cyZlay4k

 **(68) Read**
Read and enjoy an article written by Ed Hatton, **Competitive Strategy,** *http://www.entrepreneurmag.co.za/advice/business-leadership/strategy/competitive-strategy/*

 **(69) Watch:** **What is "BRAND STRATEGY"? – YouTube**
Watch this short 3:29-minute video by Gavin Wedell, W**hat is "BRAND STRATEGY"?**
https://www.youtube.com/watch?v=H-RaxV2as8s

 **(70) Read**
Read and enjoy an article written by Annetta Powell, 5 **Effective Brand Building Strategies to Attract Customers,** *http://www.coxblue.com/5-effective-brand-building-strategies-to-attract-customers-2/*

 (71) Watch: **Marketing: Positioning, Differentiation, and Value Proposition – YouTube**
Watch this short 3:29-minute video by Brain K. McCarthy, **Marketing: Positioning, Differentiation, and Value Proposition,** *https://www.youtube.com/watch?v=ugYeT3sxuQw*

 **(72) Read**

Read and enjoy an article written by Small Business Encyclopaedia, **Positioning,**
https://www.entrepreneur.com/encyclopedia/positioning

 **(73) Watch:** **What Is the Strategic Planning Process Model Steps Examples Video Lesson Transcript Studycom – YouTube**

Watch this short 4:35-minute video by Fernanda Gr, **What Is the Strategic Planning Process Model Steps Examples Video Lesson Transcript Studycom,**
https://www.youtube.com/watch?v=jVRIWeZP52k

 **(74) Read**

Read and enjoy an article written by Christoph Sisson, **Key Components of a Winning Strategic Plan,**
http://www.walsworth.com/blog/key-components-winning-strategic-plan

 **(75) Watch:** **The Secret to Strategic Implementation – YouTube**

Watch this short 3:29-minute video by Erica Olsen, **The Secret to Strategic Implementation,**
https://www.youtube.com/watch?v=ndCexCPLNdA

 **(76) Read**

Read and enjoy an article written by TCCii Strategic and Management Consultants, **Implementing A Strategic Plan Successfully,**
http://www.mondaq.com/x/140370/Operational+Performance+Management/Implementing+A+Strategic+Plan+Successfully

 **(77) Watch:** 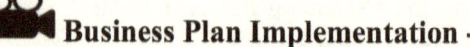 **Business Plan Implementation - YouTube**

Watch this short 2:51-minute video by Florida Buy and Sell Business Brokers, **Business Plan Implementation,**
https://www.youtube.com/watch?v=jjxG2-m436Y

 **(78) Read**

Read and enjoy an article written by Laura Click, **8 Important Steps to Successfully Implement Your Marketing Plan,**
https://flybluekite.com/how-to-implement-your-marketing-plan/

 **(79) Watch:**  **Strategic Planning: Three Keys to Successful Execution - YouTube**
Watch this 53:52-minute video by Denise Harrison, **Strategic Planning: Three Keys to Successful Execution,**
https://www.youtube.com/watch?v=-CxXQbVMYOM

 **(80) Read**
Read and enjoy an article written by Makrand Dekhane, **Strategy Implementation – Challenges,**
https://www.linkedin.com/pulse/20141210074437-19753552-strategy-implementation-challenges

 **(81) Watch:**  **Balanced Scorecard - YouTube**
Watch this short 3:59-minute video by Intrafocus as one of the monitoring elements that could lead to better control and the taking of timeous corrective actions, **Balanced Scorecard,**
https://www.youtube.com/watch?v=M_IlOlywryw&list=PLMYJuXb3F_KsOWLpYgctR2BM1yHUgu-JP

 **(82) Read**

So What's your Plan?

Read and enjoy an article written by Dr Omar Hasan Kasule, 0807- **Planning, Implementation, Control, and Evaluation,** *http://omarkasule-05.tripod.com/id329.html*

 **(83) Watch:** 10 Strategic Management: Strategy Evaluation and Control - YouTube
Watch this interesting 10:22-minute video by Executive Finance, **10 Strategic Management: Strategy Evaluation and Control,** *https://www.youtube.com/watch?v=NfKLoGZiR4s*

(84) Read and enjoy an article written by Michael Mankins and Richard Steele, **Turning Great Strategy into Great Performance,** *https://hbr.org/2005/07/turning-great-strategy-into-great-performance*

5895 M.A.S.L

www.ingramcontent.com/pod-product-compliance
Lightning Source LLC
Chambersburg PA
CBHW030629220526
45463CB00004B/1459